THE *Betty Crocker* HOME LIBRARY

Pleasures of Needlepoint

A HOW-TO BOOK OF BEAUTIFUL NEW DESIGNS
EVERYONE CAN MAKE

by Inman Cook and Daren Pierce

UNIVERSAL PUBLISHING INC. UPd NEW YORK

DISTRIBUTED BY CHARLES SCRIBNER'S SONS

Drawings by Bill Goldsmith
Photographs by Will Rousseau

Dear Friend,

For every someone who delights in "painting" on canvas with wool, there is someone else eager to start—or to graduate from kit to creative needlework.

Needlepoint has, in the past few years, taken hold in a fresh, exciting way. It has been much more than just "something to do with your hands." Today's needlepoint offers a challenge in its design, tranquility in its rhythm, and satisfaction in its completion.

To anyone who recognizes the "pleasures of needlepoint," it won't come as a surprise that this book was authored by men. After all, a famous football hero "tackles" needlepoint as enthusiastically as he tackles his opponent. And one of the country's most eminent editors is equally known for his highly original needlepoint creations.

Inman Cook and Daren Pierce traded successful careers as interior decorators to become needlepoint designers and are considered among the very top in the field. Their stitch instructions offer a sound start for the beginner and intriguing variety for the experienced. As for the projects . . . we hope you find here, not just patterns to follow, but the inspiration to "soar" on your own—to know the joy and pride of putting pattern, color, and stitches together in a thoroughly personal way.

Betty Crocker

Contents

Color Illustrations

1

The Wonderful World of Needlepoint

Anyone who can sew a basic running stitch can learn to do needle-point. Then, if you have a flair for color, a feeling for design, patience and stamina, you can create things of enduring usefulness, value, and certainly sentiment. A pillow stitched with a special motto, a hearth-rug in radiant colors, a sampler to frame for your child's bedroom—all are valued for their beauty and individuality. For the overwhelming feature of needlepoint is that it is a very personal expression; each piece is unique from corner to corner. Because the technique lends itself to hanging (a sampler) to holding (a purse), to praying (a kneeling cushion), and to padding about (bedroom slippers), it is no exaggeration to say that needlepoint's virtues are almost as endless as they are challenging.

Traditionally, you are apt to think of needlepoint in terms of the tapestries that warm church and castle walls, or of dim-colored upholstery on dining chairs, or of a bellpull that belonged to a grim old aunt. These are still beautiful to see and to marvel over, but difficult to apply to our own lives. Few of us have walls large enough for tapestries, or servants to heed the sound of a bell. Needlepoint's historic, aristocratic, and perhaps even musty, image might have remained so except for a handful of gifted artisans who, in the past decade, have boosted the craft with soaring imagination and innovation into a delightful and wholly contemporary era.

Attractive needlepoint designs can be adapted for many uses. The cushions, sunglass cases, and typewriter cover shown here are a few examples.

Modern art, with its brave new palette of colors, its anything-goes design, has had its impact. And as a result, needlepoint has been rediscovered. Many buy predesigned canvases, packaged with wool, in gaily decorated boutiques or department stores. Others, in a burst of genuine creativity, design their own canvases, and the results, as you can see from the portfolio of finished works (following page 8), are as diversified as they are inventive.

But it is wise to remind ourselves that needlepoint is not only a visual feast and a source of pleasurable products. It is also a marvelously practical hobby because it is completely portable—travels compactly anywhere, unobtrusively keeps hands busy during family chats or neighbor's visits, and is just the thing to do under the hair dryer, at the doctor's or dentist's, or to fill any "waiting" hour.

Needlepoint has still another virtue. It can be a truly reasonable pastime. (You need invest only in the canvas, needle, wool, and a bag to hold them all.) Imagination is the password here, and because imagination requires no storage space, and carries no price tag, the possibilities for design are unlimited. Learning to paint your own canvases will add to the pleasure of your work as well as educate your eye. And probably, you will never look at objects in the old way again, but as sources of inspiration for your own designs.

Think, when scavenging for patterns, of a greeting card you received in the mail, of a brightly colored, clean-lined painting, of wood grains, of dress fabrics, wallpapers, of old fireplace tiles, the cat, your favorite pastoral scene that includes a red barn shaded by a large green tree. Or think in terms of hobbies. If you collect shells, why not a series of them stitched for dining chair seats? If gardening is your consuming interest, why not scatter your favorite flowers on a bench cover? For your uncle's birthday, try a composite of his favorite things—a pipe, his dog, a fishing rod, and a golf club, to frame or take pillow shape. Can't afford an overmantel painting? Why not adapt the pattern of a favorite floral towel to your needlepoint canvas? It would make an enchanting "picture" to hang over your fireplace.

The inventiveness of needlepoint is perhaps its most enduring charm. The evening bag made in just the right pattern and colors to brighten a black dinner dress; the photograph album cover that harmonizes with the colors in your living room so that you can keep it out proudly on the coffee table; a coat for your pet dog; a gingham-patterned doorstop for your teen-age daughter's room . . . these are only a few of the one-of-a-kind things you can create to live with, or wear, or give with pride.

At its most basic, needlepoint is a craft; at its most original, it is an art form. And that is the most special of all aspects of needlepoint. It is a democratic pastime affording pleasure to the novice as well as the artist. A wall hanging and a pincushion are both keepsakes and as such, equal expressions of love and care.

Two design motifs used in a needlepoint rug. A photograph of the finished rug can be found in the color section following page 8.

Materials and Tools You Will Need

Needlepoint is really a simple form of embroidery worked on canvas with wool in a variety of stitches. You need, in addition to canvas and wool, only needles, masking tape, scissors and—this is optional—a thimble.

CANVAS

Canvas is available in various qualities. You will find the best quality a little more expensive, but it is pleasanter to work on and more durable than stiff, cheap canvases. When you buy canvas, look for an even weave and a pliable texture, and be sure that few, if any, knots are visible. Do not waste hours of effort covering an unworthy piece of material that may not last. In needlepoint as in cooking, you will get better results if you use the finest ingredients.

White single-thread canvas, or mono canvas, is the most popular variety for general use. It is available in several meshes. The number of the mesh indicates the number of threads to an inch; the basic needlepoint stitch covers an intersection of two threads on the canvas. The canvases most in demand are #10, #12, and #14 mesh.

Penelope or duo canvas is double-thread canvas and has two main advantages: petit point can be combined with regular stitching on this type of canvas by separating the two close threads; and the half-cross-stitch can be worked more easily on it. It is usually a drab ecru color (called antique) although it is sometimes made in white. The ecru is most available in #7, #9, #10, #11, #12, and #13; the white, in #7, #10, #12, and #14.

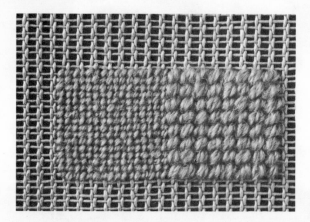

Petit point and regular stitching worked on Penelope canvas.

Mono and duo canvas can be used interchangeably unless directions specifically require one or the other. The mesh numbers of equivalents in mono and duo may vary slightly. For example, the equivalent in duo of #14 mono may be labeled #13 or #15. Don't worry about it. The difference is negligible and it will not affect your piece in any way.

Rug canvas is available in #5 mesh and #3 mesh. The name "rug" canvas, however, does not mean it is used only for rugs. It can be used for many other projects, as you will learn later in the book. If rug wool is not available, jumbo worsted or two 3-ply strands of needlepoint yarn may be substituted.

Canvas with 18 to 28 meshes per inch is called petit point canvas; with 10 to 16 meshes, gros point; and with 3 to 7 meshes, rug canvas.

Pre-printed canvas in a selection of designs is also available by the yard, in a choice of widths. The allover patterns are particularly practical for needlepoint used to cover furniture. Leftovers can be used for purses, cushions, belts, or luggage rack straps. It is much less expensive than hand-painted canvas and can be worked in many combinations of colors. Your local department store or needlework shop probably carries it.

Tassels made from yarn add decorative touches to a finished pillow.
(Instructions for making tassels are on page 113.)

The photographs that follow will show you some of the many things that can be made effectively in needlepoint. If you are a beginner, it may be wise to start by following the directions for the projects described on pages 57 to 134. When you feel confident of your needlepoint skill, leaf through these pages for ideas for other things you can make. You may want to adapt some of the designs in the projects section to these uses. Or—better still—you may be inspired to create new ideas and new designs of your own. You will soon discover that there is no end to the variety, the beauty or the pleasures of needlepoint.

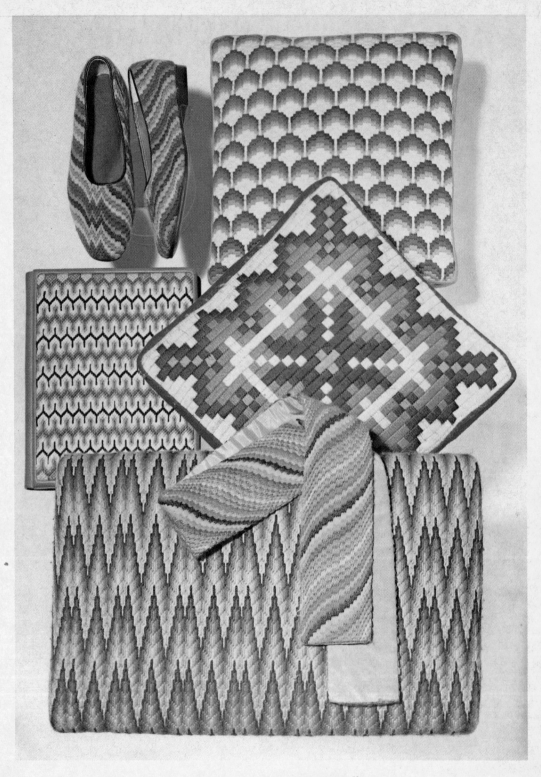

Bargello and flame-stitch patterns on slippers, pillows, a writing portfolio, a belt, and the top of a bench.

Bench upholstered in wicker pattern bargello.
(Instructions for this design are on page 94.)

A fireplace screen with a flame-stitch panel.

A Charles X design rug worked in squares. The all-over pattern is achieved by repeating two design motifs. The border is worked separately, using another design repeated along the edges and a fourth motif in the four corners.

A variety of needlepoint articles. The stylized version of a Cheshire Cat is framed; the dog's coat is a design of Chinese clouds; the vest is worked in a bargello design; the wastebasket matches a curtain fabric; the dimensional geometric design bordered in suede was adapted from a fresco in a cathedral in France; the red and white pillow is another bargello design.

Needlepoint patterns adapted from wallpaper and fabric designs.

A tea-box pattern is an effective geometric as shown in the tote bag below.

Poppy design. Colors can be changed
to complement your color scheme.

Needlepoint can be witty as well as serious. This cherry pie pillow using a lattice-work design is a good example.

Needlepoint pillows add color and pattern to a room.

WOOL

Wool that is used for needlepoint should have strong, long fibers that do not stretch. Knitting or crewel wools are not recommended because their stretching and contracting tend to pull the canvas out of shape.

Several wools are made expressly for needlepoint, and the choice of which to use is a personal one. So-called "Persian" wool is popular because it is available in an extensive range of colors and because of its versatility. It comes in "3-ply," which means that it is made up of three strands twisted together. These strands can be separated so that you can use a single strand, a double strand, or the full 3-ply, depending on the mesh of the canvas.

Persian wool is sold in large or small skeins or by the ounce, usually cut into 30-inch strands. You can buy as many strands as you need, which is particularly economical when you want to do just a few stitches in one color.

Tapestry yarn or needlepoint wool is a 4-ply wool that is usually sold in skeins ranging from 8.8 to 15 yards per skein. It is sometimes available in 100-yard and 180-yard skeins. The number of yards is always printed on the wrapper so that if you want to buy the equivalent of one ounce of Persian wool in tapestry yarn just remember that one ounce of Persian equals 40 yards; a half ounce, 20 yards. Figure the number of skeins of tapestry yarn you need accordingly.

Tapestry yarn is almost always used in full 4-ply because it is rather difficult to separate the strands. It is softer than Persian, however, and in most cases 4-ply tapestry yarn can be substituted for 3-ply, or even 2-ply, Persian.

Needleworkers may use other types of yarns, too, such as acrylic or nylon. Some very effective pieces have also been made using giant, jumbo, or colossal worsted on rug canvas. It is not advisable to use cotton or rayon rug yarn.

Rug wool has a coarse texture and is approximately the diameter of a wooden pencil. It is used singly on #5 mesh canvas and cross-stitched on #3 mesh canvas. An ounce of rug wool is approximately 15⅓ yards; a strand is 30 inches. Acrylic rug yarn comes in skeins or balls. A 1¾ ounce skein is about 60 yards; a ball is about 52 yards.

It is difficult to be precise in figuring the amount of wool needed for any given piece of needlepoint because of personal variations in working. The tightness or looseness of the stitch and the wastefulness or thrift exercised in ending threads can make a difference in the amount of yarn used. But don't try to be too frugal. It is a waste of time to attempt to eke out the very last inch of wool. Leave a piece long enough to work through a few stitches on the back and cut it off!

If you are working an original design, take it or mail it to your source of materials, where a professional can judge the amount of wool required. If this is impossible, work one square inch of canvas and keep track of how much wool you used. Multiply this by the number of square inches in each color section (or approximate it), then add a few extra yards to allow for errors. Buy enough wool for the background when you start so that you are sure it is all from the same dye lot. Dye lots seldom, if ever, match exactly.

NEEDLES AND A FEW OTHER THINGS

Blunt-nosed needles called tapestry needles are made expressly for needlepoint and are available in a variety of sizes. Wool and needles to coordinate with some popular meshes are listed below:

Canvas	Wool	Needle Size
#3 mesh	Rug wool (or jumbo, giant, or colossal worsted or acrylic yarn)	#13 rug needle
#5 mesh	Rug wool (or jumbo, giant, or colossal worsted or acrylic yarn)	#13 rug needle
#10 mesh	Full 3-ply Persian (or full tapestry yarn)	#17
#12 mesh	2-ply Persian* (or full tapestry yarn)	#18
#14 mesh	2-ply Persian* (or full tapestry yarn)	#19

*For bargello, use full 3-ply on this mesh.

You can be flexible in choosing the size of the needle except when you use rug wool or work with silk on very fine mesh canvas. A #17 or #18 needle can be used on most other projects.

Masking or Adhesive Tape

Tape is used to bind the raw edges of the canvas so they do not ravel as you work. The types used for this purpose are usually from 1 inch to 1½ inches wide. Masking tape can be purchased in stationery, variety, hardware, or art supply stores; adhesive tape is available in variety stores, drugstores, and in many supermarkets.

Scissors and Thimble

Small, sharp embroidery scissors or curved manicure scissors; a thimble, if you are so inclined; and perseverance are the other basic requirements for a venture into the pleasures of needlepoint.

SOURCES OF MATERIALS

Some needlepoint shops and department stores sell only packaged designs or their own original hand-painted canvases. Many shops around the country, however, sell canvas by the yard and wool either by the ounce or by the skein. Consult the Yellow Pages in your telephone directory. These shops are listed under *Art Needlework, Art Needlework Materials, Yarns,* or *Wool.*

3 ∽

Designing Needlepoint

You may have a picture in mind of what a needlepoint design looks like, or *should* look like. Bouquets and border designs were once almost the only options for needlework pieces. That is no longer the case. Given some basic guidelines, you can create and execute designs of almost any kind in needlepoint.

The end use of the needlepoint piece should be the main influence in the selection of its design, and the finished needlepoint should be suitable to the kind of wear for which it is intended. For instance, a man's vest suggests a pattern quite different from a pillow or a picture for a little girl's room. Objects for the home should, of course, be compatible in color and design with other elements of its decoration.

ADAPTING DESIGNS

Designs from wallpaper and fabric can be adapted for chair seats or pillows by tracing the whole pattern or by selecting one motif from the pattern. (See photograph following page 8.) If necessary, the design can be photostated up or down to whatever size is desired. (If you choose an allover design or a large-scale motif, you will have less background to fill in and the work will be more interesting.)

TRANSFERRING DESIGNS

There are two methods of transferring an original, traced, or adapted design to canvas: one way is to draw it on a graph-paper chart; the other is to paint it directly on the canvas. The graph-paper chart method is perhaps the simpler of the two.

Graph-paper Charts

Select a piece of canvas 2½ inches wider all around than the finished needlepoint piece is to be. Use masking or adhesive tape to bind the edges firmly so the threads will not ravel. Mark the outline of the area to be worked in the center of the canvas. Count the number of *threads* in the working area of the canvas from left to right and from top to bottom. Count the same number of *squares* on the graph paper and draw in the outline of the canvas. Each square on the paper represents one stitch on the canvas. The size of the graph-paper squares may be entirely different from that of the mesh of the canvas, so don't be alarmed if the outline on the graph-paper doesn't resemble the actual size of the finished piece. The relation of square to stitch remains the same. Sketch the design on the graph paper, ignoring the graph lines. Next, draw the major outlines, following the graph paper's lines as closely as possible. You will find that curves and circles are impossible to reproduce in needlepoint, but a stairstep effect (as shown below) will create the illusion of a curve or circle in the finished work.

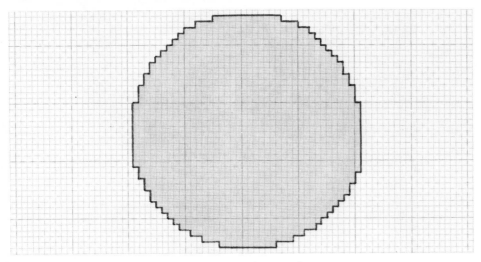

Block in the design with colored pencils or markers to serve as a color guide.

If the design is placed on the graph paper in exactly the position you want it on the finished product you can begin your needlepoint anywhere on the canvas. Count the squares on the graph paper and duplicate each square with a stitch on the canvas. If you have miscalculated and the design is not centered on the graph paper, measure and mark the center of the designed area. Fold the canvas in four to find its center. Begin the stitches there with the stitch that is in the center of the graph. Work outward, counting the squares on the graph, and the design will center itself.

Mottoes, Monograms, and Geometric Designs

Lettering, monograms, mottoes, and geometric designs are especially suited to the graph-paper method of transferring designs to canvas. They can be used on any mesh canvas by counting the same number of stitches on the canvas as are shown on the graph paper.

In planning a motto or monogram, it is best to do a layout on graph paper copying the letters from the alphabets on pages 78, 126-128. Then you can see if the placement is pleasing and correct. Even with experience, it is almost impossible to place the letters correctly the first time. A paper layout also helps you cope with the absolute physical limitations of how much lettering will go into a given space. If you are working within a definitely defined area, mark the size on the canvas and count the threads up and down and from side to side. Count the same number of squares on the graph paper and make an outline. Since each square represents a stitch, you soon realize that the Lord's Prayer cannot be put on a pincushion!

To transfer lettering or geometric designs from graph paper to canvas, use a waterproof marker or a small brush with acrylic paint thinned with water. Mark one intersection of threads (one stitch) on the canvas for each square on the graph paper.

If you want to enlarge the letters, substitute four stitches instead of a single stitch for each square on the chart. In fact, any geometric pattern can be enlarged by substituting four stitches for one square on the chart. The scale of the design also depends on the canvas mesh.

The same geometric design worked on #12 mesh canvas will be four times larger if it is worked on #3 mesh canvas.

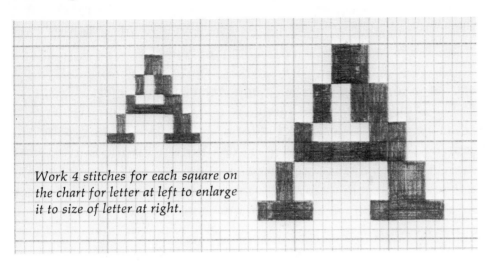

Work 4 stitches for each square on the chart for letter at left to enlarge it to size of letter at right.

Painting Designs on Canvas

The other way to transfer a design is to paint it directly on the needlepoint canvas. Painting requires a certain skill but is certainly not beyond the ability of the average person if a few guidelines are followed. Painting on the canvas is more practical if the design is free in its execution. This method also eliminates the necessity for carrying the graph paper around and counting squares while working the piece.

Mark the outline of the finished needlepoint piece on drawing or tracing paper. Lightly sketch in the design with pencil, then paint in the desired colors on the paper. The paint may sink through, so put something under the paper to protect the work surface.

Mark the outline of the finished piece on the canvas, leaving at least 2½ inches of canvas free of design all around for finishing. Bind the edges with masking or adhesive tape to prevent raveling.

When the paper design is thoroughly dry, tape it to a table or drawing board and place the canvas over it so that the outlines of the design coincide. Tape the canvas down to keep it from slipping. Now trace the design onto the canvas and paint in the colors.

Felt-tip markers or acrylic paints are the most practical mediums for transferring a design to needlepoint canvas and are available at most art supply shops or stationery stores. Felt-tip markers *must* be waterproof so that the colors will not run into the wool when the piece is dampened for blocking. Acrylic paint should be thinned with water to keep it from clogging the holes of the canvas. Markers and acrylic paint dry almost at once. Oil paint thinned with turpentine can be used, but it has the disadvantage of drying slowly, and of course it must be *thoroughly* dry before the needlepoint is started.

If the design is floral or free-form, in other words, not geometric, it is not necessary to pay too much attention to the canvas mesh when painting on the design. The effect will be achieved in the finished needlepoint. However, the painted design should be used as a general outline; you can improve the design by adding detail while working it. In almost all cases it is better to work a stitch or two beyond the design outline than to cramp the stitches within the outline.

If art work in any form is not your strong point, hand-painted canvases are available across the country and by mail order at various prices. Usually they are packaged in kits with the wool and the needles required to work them.

The Yellow Pages in your telephone directory are a good source for companies that supply kits directly or by mail order. Look under *Art Needlework*.

ENLARGING AND REDUCING DESIGNS

You can enlarge a design by using canvas with a lower mesh count to the inch. A design worked on #14 mesh is 1⅝ inches square and the same design cross-stitched on #3 mesh is 7⅔ inches square, although the same number of stitches is used. You can also make a design smaller by using a canvas with more squares to the inch. For example, if a 14-inch square pattern is designed for #10 mesh canvas, by working the same design on #12 mesh, the completed piece will be 11⅔ inches.

In working the projects that follow (starting on page 58), it is important to use the mesh specified if you want the finished pieces to be the size given in the directions.

The same design worked on different canvas meshes. From left to right: #3, #5, #10, #12, #14. This shows how the size, texture, and character of the design are altered by changing the size of the mesh.

4 ∾

Some Tips Before You Start

As some cookbooks say, "First, wash your hands." It may sound like unnecessary advice, but a soiled thread will stick out like a sore thumb when the piece is finished.

When *measuring the amount of canvas you need*, always allow 2 or 2½ extra inches of canvas all around the outline of your piece to allow for blocking and finishing.

Before you start stitching, *bind the edges* of the canvas with masking or adhesive tape to prevent raveling.

If there is a *selvage* on the canvas, keep it at one side, not at the top or bottom.

Occasionally *a thread or two in the canvas may appear slightly crooked or out of line.* You may be able to even it out with your fingernail or needle before you start to stitch. Even if all the threads seem to slant slightly, don't panic. After the piece is worked and blocked it won't be noticeable. However, *if the canvas is badly out of line,* you would be wiser not to use it as you would be wasting valuable time and money on a piece that will never look quite right.

Persian wool cut into 30-inch strands comes loosely knotted in the center. Do not untie the knot. As you need a strand, gently draw it from the knot. *A large skein* of Persian wool can be cut at each end to make 30-inch strands. Be sure to tie the strands into a loose knot and follow directions above. If you buy *a small skein* of Persian or any size skein of tapestry or needlepoint wool, leave the paper band on it and pull out the yarn as needed. Or, if you prefer, you can wind the wool into a ball as you would for knitting.

For regular needlepoint, your working wool should be about 30 inches long (or less), so that it will not fray as it is pulled in and out of the canvas. Rug wool can be longer, up to 60 inches, because it is used up very quickly.

To thread the needle, place it under the wool about 3 or 4 inches from an end. Pinch the wool tightly around the needle and extract the needle, leaving a tight flat loop. Press the eye down on the loop and the wool will pop through. Pull it all the way through and the

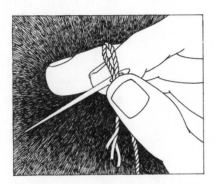

needle is threaded. If this method does not work for you, resort to a needle threader or the "paper method." Cut a 2- or 3-inch strip of firm paper a little narrower than the width of the needle's eye. Fold it in half and insert it through the eye, making a paper loop on the other side. Place the end of the wool in the loop, and pull it back through the needle. This method is also useful if your wool escapes from the needle when you are at the end of a piece of wool and want to tuck the remaining inch or two through the stitches on the back.

Needlepoint wool should never be knotted. *To begin a stitch,* bring the threaded needle up from the back of the canvas, allowing an inch or two of wool to remain at the back. Hold the piece of wool at the back, and manipulate it with your fingers so that it is gradually bound under with the first few stitches. When the end is firmly worked in, snip off any wool that is left over. Always keep the back of the work neatly trimmed in this way. If you leave ends hanging from the back they inevitably fuzz their way through to the front.

Begin your needlepoint in the upper right-hand corner when working the continental or basket-weave method (because these stitches must be worked from right to left).

If the piece you are working on is large, keep the unworked portion rolled up and pinned so that it will be easier to hold. The canvas may seem stiff at first, but it will soften as you work with it.

As you do the stitches, *keep the wool relaxed.* If the stitches are pulled too tight, the canvas will show through and the piece will be stretched completely out of shape. When you have worked about half of the length of a piece of wool, drop the needle, allowing it to hang loose, and its weight will untwist the wool. This will help to keep the wool relaxed and the stitches more even.

To finish a piece of wool, run the needle under five or six of the just-completed stitches on the back of the canvas and snip off the tag end. To start the next piece of wool, bury it for about three-quarters of an inch through the worked section on the back and bring it forward where you want to start the next stitch. Use this same method when you change colors or begin a new area of the design.

When you are working a design in which several small areas of one color are near each other, you need not snip off the wool after completing each small group of stitches. Simply go from one group to the next. The short lengths of wool joining these areas on the back will be covered later by the background stitches.

However, *if the next group of stitches in the same color is more than an inch away,* run the end of the wool into a few of the completed stitches on the back; trim off the end; and treat the next group as a separate design area. If there is still a generous amount of yarn left on your needle, it is a good idea to tie it (still threaded on the needle) loosely around the handle of the bag that holds your wool so it is readily seen and available when you need it for the next area in that color.

If you discover a mistake, rip out the stitches necessary to correct the error. It is best to unthread the needle and use it to pull each stitch out. Do not try to undo the stitches by putting the threaded needle back through the hole as it is liable to get caught through other wool and end up knotted. If the mistake is more than one full row back, it may be faster to snip each stitch with sharp, pointed scissors. However, there is always the danger of cutting into the canvas, so be *very* careful if you do it this way.

When the needlepoint is completed, look over the entire piece carefully to be sure you have not missed a stitch here and there. If you have, it is an easy matter to locate the position on the back, lock the wool under a few stitches, bring the needle out, and cover the missed stitch.

It is best to *work the design first* and then the background. If the background is white, be sure to trim the ends of the colored wool in the design neatly before you start to work the background. White wool tends to pick up filaments that give the piece a muddy look or make it appear that the color has run into the white. Once this has happened nothing can be done to correct the effect. Keeping the colored ends out of the way will avoid this discoloration. Of course, if you are transferring a design to canvas and can see the outline of the design clearly, it is possible, and desirable, to work a white background *before* you do the design to avoid the pickup of color. If the white background gets a little soiled from handling, you can always freshen it when the piece is finished by brushing the surface lightly with a cloth dipped in a good cleaning fluid.

If a white line of canvas shows when you turn back the margin of a worked piece, overcast the edge with yarn using the background color.

When glue is needed in finishing, use an all-purpose glue such as Sobo or Elmer's glue.

It is advisable to *keep all your needlepoint paraphernalia in some kind of a bag* so that it will stay clean and always be available to carry with you.

Keep a plastic bag handy to save leftover wool that can be used for another project.

5 ⌒

Needlepoint Stitches

If you have the urge to learn and the patience to practice, you can master the basic needlepoint stitches by following the step-by-step instructions and diagrams on the next few pages. It will save you time and effort if someone who knows needlepoint can help you get started, but whether you learn with personal guidance or from this book alone, you will be surprised at how quickly you can be on your way to enjoying the pleasures of needlepoint.

The instructions will help you learn the actual mechanics of several needlepoint stitches. With practice, you will be able to do these stitches easily and rhythmically without even thinking about the mechanics involved.

The best way to learn is by doing. Don't attempt to read the instructions without having a piece of canvas and a needle threaded with yarn in your hand so you can follow each step as you go along. Use a piece of #10 mesh canvas and full 3-ply wool or full tapestry yarn with a #17 or #18 needle. A piece about 12 inches square will give you plenty of room to try all the stitches described here. If you want to practice further before you start on any of the projects, work several rows of each stitch until you feel the rhythm of it. Some beginners work a four-inch square of each stitch for practice. Allow a 2-inch margin of canvas all around. If the square turns out well, it can be blocked, finished, and used as a coaster or a small pad for a hot plate.

Note: *In needlepoint instructions, the space in the canvas where the needle goes in or comes out is referred to as a* square *or a* hole. *The terms are used interchangeably. A* mesh *is a thread. For example, #10, or 10-mesh canvas, is woven with 10 threads to the inch.*

If you are left-handed and a beginner at needlepoint, you should first try to learn the stitches using your right hand. Awkwardness, initially, may be from inexperience rather than from being left-handed. If this does not work for you, try following all of the stitch directions backwards or directly opposite from the way they read. For example, if the directions say to begin in the upper right-hand corner, begin in the lower left-hand corner of the project instead. If the directions say to work from right to left, you work from left to right. If the directions say to insert the needle 1 square to the right in the row above, you insert it 1 square to the left in the row below. In following the directions, always substitute the words "right" for "left," "left" for "right," "top" for "bottom," "bottom" for "top," "lower" for "upper," and "upper" for "lower."

Actually there are no iron-clad rules in creative work. Guidelines based on experience can be offered and will prove helpful during the learning period. There are a few basic stitches and literally hundreds of variations. The choice really depends on what will bring you the most enjoyment and accomplish the effect you want.

It may cheer you to keep in mind that most contemporary needlepoint patterns depend upon mass effect rather than complicated stitch techniques. You will be amazed at the effects you can achieve with a few simple stitches.

TENT STITCH

The tent stitch is the basic stitch used in needlepoint. It is a diagonal stitch worked on an angle over an intersection of canvas threads from the lower left-hand square to the upper right. There are three methods for working this stitch: the *continental method*, the *half-cross method* (with *cross-stitch* variation), and the *basket-weave method*. Each method represents a different way of accomplishing the same result. Each forms a tent stitch on the face of the canvas. Work in the method you find easiest and most comfortable to do, and the one best suited to the canvas and design you are using.

CONTINENTAL METHOD

This is probably the most widely used method of working the tent stitch. It is easy to learn, covers well, provides a padded back, and can be done on either mono or duo (Penelope) canvas. It is also the stitch used for petit point. The stitch is always worked from right to left which means that the canvas must be inverted as each line is finished. When this method is used over an entire piece, it tends to pull the canvas out of shape. However, the worked piece can be stretched back to the original dimensions by blocking. (See page 55.)

All stitches should slant in the same direction, so before beginning, decide which is the "top" of the canvas and mark it "top." Always hold the canvas in this position, or in the directly opposite or "bottom" position. Never work with one of the sides of the canvas at the top.

Start at the upper right-hand corner of the color area to be covered. Begin the stitch by bringing the needle up from the back of the canvas, allowing about an inch of wool to remain at the back. Hold the piece of wool on the back with your finger, and bind it under as you do the first few stitches.

The 1st stitch is made by inserting the needle 1 square to the right in the row above and bringing it out in the square to the left of where the 1st stitch began. This gives you a diagonal stitch that crosses one intersection of canvas threads.

Proceed from right to left across the canvas to the end of the area you wish to cover. Leaving the needle on the back of the canvas, turn the canvas around so that the top is at the bottom. Insert the needle below and to the left of the intersection to be covered, and proceed back across the canvas. The continental method is always used when working a single line in a design.

To make a vertical line, begin at the top and work down. Bring the needle up from the back of the canvas. Insert the needle 1 square to the right in the row above, bring it out in the square directly below where the 1st stitch started. The 2nd stitch in the vertical line is made in the same manner. Insert the needle 1 square to the right in the row above, and bring it out in the square directly below where the 2nd stitch started. Continue the vertical line down in the same way.

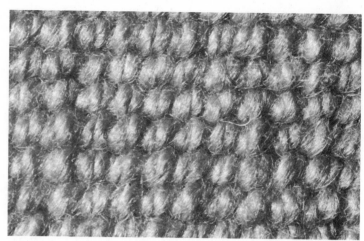

HALF-CROSS METHOD

The half-cross tent is sometimes referred to as the "cheap stitch" because it uses less wool than the other methods. It should be worked on Penelope (duo) canvas. The double threads of the canvas make it firm, allowing you to make completed stitches without moving your hand from front to back of the canvas with every stitch as you must do with this stitch if you use mono.

The half-cross method is not recommended for any piece that will receive hard usage, except for rugs or upholstery worked with rug wool on #5 mesh canvas. In this case it is desirable because there is much less wool on the back than if any other stitch were used. The piece will be thinner and therefore more workable. Like the continental method, the half-cross tends to pull the canvas out of shape, but blocking will stretch the finished piece back to its original contour.

Work the half-cross stitch from left to right, beginning at the upper left-hand corner of the color area to be covered. The half-cross is worked with the needle vertical at all times. Bring the needle up from the back of the canvas, allowing about an inch of wool to remain at the back. It must be manipulated with your finger so that it will be locked in by subsequent stitches.

To make the 1st stitch, insert the needle 1 square to the right in the row above, and bring it out through the square directly below. You have crossed one intersection of threads with a diagonal stitch slanting upward from left to right. The 2nd and subsequent stitches

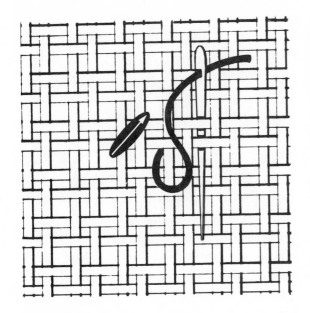 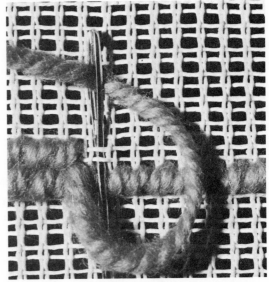

are made in the same manner, until the row is finished. Because it is worked in rows across the area to be covered, the canvas should be inverted at the end of each row in order to work back again.

CROSS-STITCH VARIATION

The cross-stitch variation is a double version of the half-cross method. Two diagonal stitches of yarn form an X, the 1st slanting from lower left to upper right and the 2nd from lower right to upper left. The top stitches should slant in the same direction. This stitch bears very little resemblance to an embroidered cross-stitch. It looks more like a heavy, padded stitch than a cross.

This method is suggested for #5 mesh canvas and is *required* to fill in #3 mesh canvas with rug yarn. It is particularly desirable for geometric patterns as the stitch itself forms a square.

Because this method is customarily used for rugs, it is important to mark the "top" of a square and to hold the canvas in a top-up position or directly opposite in a bottom-up position. This precaution is to insure that all the stitches slant in the same direction. Never work with one of the sides of the canvas at the top.

There are two ways of working the cross-stitch. One method is to half-cross stitch an entire row from left to right and then work back over the same line to complete the crosses. This way seems preferable for filling in backgrounds. The second method is to complete each cross-stitch, one at a time. This is preferred for small areas.

When forming a stitch, try to avoid putting the needle through an adjacent piece of yarn. It tends to distort the stitch and makes it nearly impossible to remove the stitches in case of error.

First method: Starting in the upper left-hand corner, bring the needle up from the back of the canvas. Leave about an inch of wool at the back; hold it on the back with your finger and manipulate it so that it is bound under by the first few stitches.

To make the 1st stitch, insert the needle 1 square to the right in the row above and bring it out through the square directly below (diagram 1). Be careful not to pull too tight. The 2nd and subsequent stitches are made in the same way until the end of the row is reached.

It is now time to cross each stitch working back over them. Insert the needle 1 square to the left in the row above; bring it out directly below (diagram 2). You will be covering the same "tracks" as before but in the opposite direction. Continue in this way until each stitch in the row has been crossed.

Second method: To complete each cross as you go along, start in the upper right corner of the area to be covered. Bring the needle up from the back, and bind in the tag end as explained before.

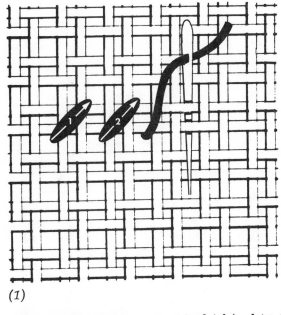

(1)

First method: Work a row in half-cross, then complete the crosses.

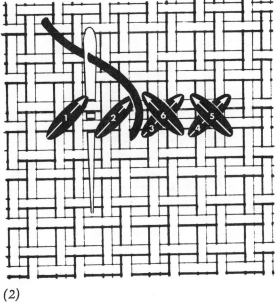

(2)

The 1st stitch is made by inserting the needle 1 square to the right in the row above and bringing it out in the square directly below. Now insert the needle 1 square to the left in the row above and bring it out diagonally 1 square to the left in the row below. The

Second method: Complete each cross as you go along.

subsequent stitches are made in the same way. At the end of the row, invert the canvas so that the top stitch in each cross will slant in the same direction on the 2nd row as it did on the first.

To work from top to bottom, lock in the tag end as before. Insert the needle 1 square to the right in the row above and bring it out in the square directly below. Next, insert the needle 1 square to the left in the row above and bring it out through the 2nd square directly below, skipping the worked square. Proceed down the canvas. Invert the canvas at the end of each row so that all the top stitches will slant in the same direction.

Front   *Back*

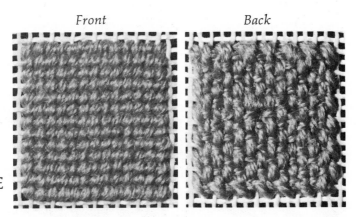

BASKET-WEAVE METHOD

From the front, basket weave looks the same as continental. The name comes from the basket-weave effect the wool forms on the reverse side. This method has several advantages over the continental. It does not pull the canvas out of shape as much; it does not require turning the canvas around at the end of every row; it forms a sturdy and padded back; and it seems to fill in faster than other methods. (Note: it cannot be used for outlines or single lines.)

The basket weave is worked from right to left but fills in diagonally rather than in horizontal rows. Bring the needle up from the back of the canvas, holding about an inch of wool at the back with your finger and binding it under with the first few stitches.

Starting at the upper right-hand corner of the color area to be covered, work 3 stitches to establish the diagonal. The *1st stitch* of the diagonal is made by inserting the needle 1 square to the right in the row above and bringing it out in the square to the left of where the 1st stitch began. The *2nd stitch* is made by inserting the needle 1 square to the right in the row above. Hold the needle in a vertical position, skip the 1st worked stitch and bring the needle out in the square directly below where the 1st stitch began. To make the *3rd stitch*, insert the needle 1 square to the right in the row above. Hold the needle in a diagonal position and bring it out in the square directly below where the 3rd stitch began. You have now established the diagonal.

Now begin working *up the ladder* diagonally from right to left. To make the 4th and 5th stitches, work with the needle in a horizontal position, always inserting it in the next upper right square, skipping the worked square, and bringing it out in the 2nd square to the left (diagram 1). When you work up the ladder, the wool on the back is *horizontal*.

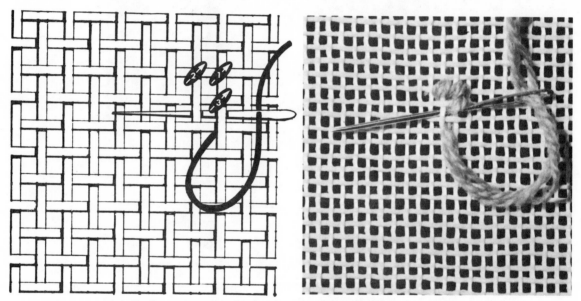

(1) Basket-weave Method: 4th stitch, starting up the ladder

The 6th stitch is a *turn-around stitch* so you can start working back down the ladder. Insert the needle in a diagonal position into the upper right-hand square and bring it out in the square directly to the left of where the 6th stitch began (diagram 2).

Now start working *down the ladder* diagonally from left to right. Insert the needle in the upper right-hand square. Holding the needle in a vertical position, skip the worked stitch, and bring it out in the unworked square below (diagram 3). Continue down the ladder in

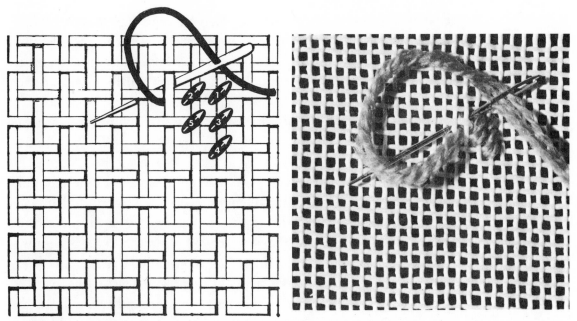

(2) Basket-weave Method: 6th (turn-around) stitch

this way. When you work down the ladder, the wool on the back is *vertical*.

When you reach the bottom of this diagonal, the 10th stitch will be another turn-around stitch, a diagonal one. Insert the needle in the upper right-hand square and bring it out in the unworked square *directly below* where the stitch began. You are now ready to work with the needle in a horizontal position back up the ladder.

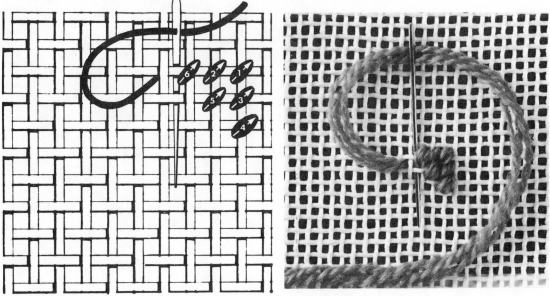

(3) Basket-weave Method: 7th stitch, starting down the ladder

Remember that whenever you reach the end of a diagonal row, or the edge of a color area, you must make a turn-around stitch before changing direction. At first, you may have to remind yourself to make these turn-around stitches, but with a little practice they become as automatic as the rest.

Another important thing to keep in mind is that all stitches should slant in the same direction.

When you work a piece in the basket-weave method, sooner or later it becomes necessary for you to begin on a section of background which was left behind when the design interrupted it. It is important to look at the back of the canvas and be sure to continue the background so that the "basket weave" is maintained. (See photograph on page 31.) That is, if the last completed ladder was horizontal, the next should be vertical. Vertical stitches on the back of the canvas are created when you start at the top and work down the ladder, horizontal ones by starting at the bottom and working up the ladder. If this rule is not followed, a ridge will show on the front of the canvas.

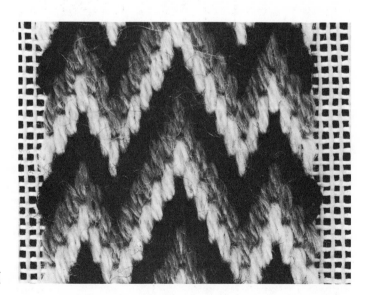

FLAME STITCH

One of the easiest and yet most fascinating stitches in needlepoint is the flame stitch, so named because the many variations of zigzag designs that can be made with it resemble flames. The stitch can be used in an endless variety of patterns and once the basic stitch is mastered, new designs can be created. (This style of needle-point is also called bargello although bargello patterns are not always flamelike.)

Flame stitch is made by skipping holes in the canvas. Many of the patterns skip 3 holes, so it is easy to see that it takes only about one-third of the time that would be needed to stitch each hole indi-vidually. The stitches are worked vertically, not diagonally as is customary with many other needlepoint stitches.

The most practical mesh of canvas for flame stitch is #14 mono. Three full plys of Persian wool or full tapestry yarn should be used. However, some effective pieces can be made quickly using a larger mesh canvas, such as #5 and either a single or double strand of jumbo yarn.

There are two important things to remember when you do the flame stitch. First, keep the yarn soft and relaxed. If the yarn is pulled too tightly, or if it is twisted, the canvas will show through. This is particularly true when you use a large mesh canvas. Second, and this point cannot be emphasized enough, when you discover a mistake, find the root of it at once, rip it out back to its origin, and correct it. One unheeded mistake will grow in magnitude until the design is completely ruined. If these two precautions are kept in mind, flame stitching should be smooth sailing.

Before you start to do the flame stitch or any bargello stitch, it is important to learn how to count "holes up" or "holes down." If you ignore the worked hole when you start counting you will have no problem. For example, when directions read "insert the needle in the third hole up," start counting with the hole *above* the worked hole. If the directions read "bring the needle up through the second hole down," start counting with the hole *below* the worked hole. The same method applies to counting horizontal and vertical rows. Here, too, all you have to remember is to start counting with the nearest, unworked row.

Flame stitch is based on a design repeat system, so as soon as the basic pattern is set up, the filling in is almost automatic.

A monochromatic color scheme seems most suitable for either contemporary or traditional decor: three shades of blue and white; three shades of gold and white; four shades of green; dark reds shading to pink. These are only a few suggestions from an almost endless palette. Contrasting colors can be effective too, especially in small pieces. In any case, the colors should be coordinated with other fabrics in the room if the piece is to be used for pillows or upholstery.

The simplest pattern for beginners is the zigzag flame, which is also one of the most attractive and usable. With a zigzag flame pattern it is usually best to start in the center of the canvas and work out, so that the peak of a flame will be centered on the piece. You can begin in the exact center of the canvas or at the bottom center.

The 1st stitch will be the lowest part of the flame pattern (an inverted V) because it is easier to work up to a peak than to work down to its base.

Bring the needle from back to front leaving about an inch of yarn to be locked in by the first few stitches. The stitch is taken straight upward, skipping 3 holes and entering the 4th. Bring the needle back out to the front in the 1st row to the right, through the 2nd hole down. Working upward, skip 3 holes, enter the 4th, and bring the needle back to the front in the next row to the right through the 2nd hole down.

For a very simple pattern, to practice the stitch, repeat this side-stepping up for 2 more stitches, complete the 4th stitch so that the needle is at the front of the canvas (in the 2nd hole down), then invert the canvas.

Continue working in an upward direction, but now from right to left. Insert the needle in the 4th hole up and bring it out in the 1st row to the left through the 2nd hole down. Repeat the sidestepping twice more, and the stitches will have formed a V. The needle should be at the front of the canvas.

Invert the canvas and work upward from left to right again for 3 stitches. Invert the canvas and work upward from right to left for 3 stitches. Repeat the 4-stitch-peaks to the edge of the piece. Run the yarn under an inch of worked stitches on the back and cut off the end.

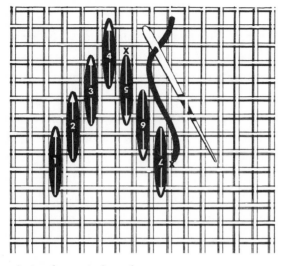

A simple 4-stitch peak

Turn the canvas so that the 1st stitch is again bottom center. Run the yarn under an inch of worked stitches on the back and bring the needle out in the row to the left of the 1st stitch through the 2nd hole up. Repeat the 4-stitch-peaks to the opposite side of the canvas. The basic flame pattern is now set up.

A combination of 5-stitch and 3-stitch peaks.

The next gradation of color should be used in the 2nd row across. The new color and row can be started from either side. Lock the yarn through the stitches on the back and bring the needle to the front of the canvas through the top hole of the stitch below in the 1st row worked. All horizontal canvas threads must be covered. Complete the 2nd line across the canvas, following the patterns of the 1st.

The 3rd row should be worked in the next gradation of color and so on until the canvas is covered. This row (and subsequent rows) can be started above or below the completed rows.

Cautions worth repeating: Leave the wool relaxed and do not pull it too tightly. If you make a mistake, rip it out!

Note: *The diagram shown here is a drawing of a piece of canvas. On a chart for a flame-stitch design, each square represents a horizontal thread to be covered. Therefore, when the instruction in a flame-stitch design is to bring the needle to the front of the canvas, skip 3 holes and enter the 4th; although 5 holes are involved in making the stitch, only 4 squares (4 threads) are covered in the chart. (See chart for Flame-stitch Eyeglass Case on page 64.)*

GOBELIN STITCH

The Gobelin stitch is very useful for background work. Like the flame stitch, it is made by skipping holes, so the work goes much faster than it does with the tent stitch. It also offers a contrast in texture from a design motif worked in the tent stitch. Gobelin, which gives a ribbed effect, is worked straight across the canvas rather than in the sidestepping manner of the flame stitch. It can be made by skipping 1, 2, or 3 holes, depending on how pronounced you wish the ribbed effect to be.

Full 3-ply Persian or full tapestry yarn is used for Gobelin stitching. It must be left very loose, or the canvas will show through.

The Gobelin stitch is worked from right to left. Begin in the upper right-hand corner. Bring the needle up from the back of the canvas. Hold about an inch of wool at the back with your finger, and bind it under with the first few stitches.

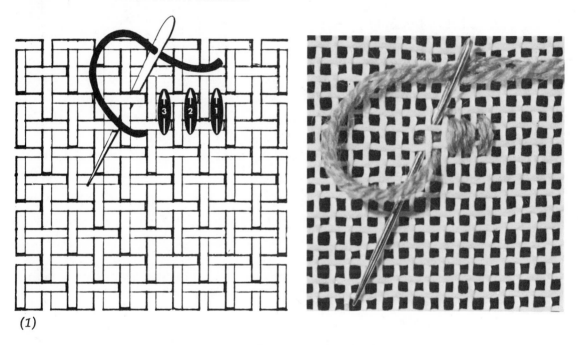

(1)

In diagram 1 above, the 1st stitch is made by skipping 1 hole, inserting the needle in the 2nd hole directly above and bringing it out through the 2nd hole down, one row to the left. This same stitch is repeated across the canvas. At the end of the row, leave the needle at the back of the canvas inserted in the top row.

For *the 2nd row*, invert the canvas and bring the needle to the surface through the same hole as what is now the top of the last stitch.

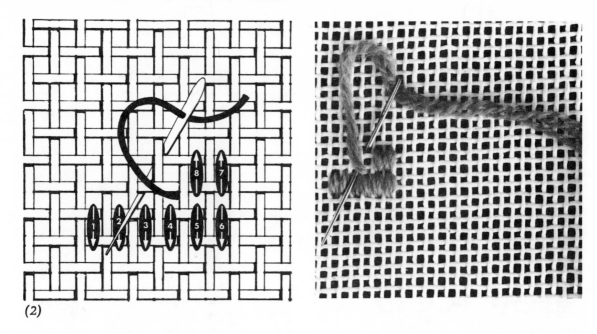

(2)

Insert the needle in the 2nd hole directly above, and bring it out in the square to the left of where the previous stitch began (diagram 2). Continue back across the canvas in this manner. At the end of the row, leave the needle at the back of the canvas inserted in the top row.

To do *the 3rd row*, invert the canvas and bring the needle to the front through the 2nd hole down from your last stitch. Insert the needle in the 2nd hole directly above and work back across the canvas. All horizontal threads must be covered.

Note: *On a chart for a design using Gobelin (or Slanting Gobelin) each square represents a horizontal thread covered.*

SLANTING GOBELIN STITCH

The slanting Gobelin stitch is almost like the straight Gobelin stitch and gives practically the same ribbed effect for background work. It has the advantage of covering the canvas more thoroughly. It is done exactly as in the continental method, except that instead of inserting the needle 1 square to the right *1* row above, you insert the needle 1 square to the right *2* rows above (or 3, or 4, or 5, depending on the length you want the stitch to be). Use full 3-ply Persian or full tapestry yarn.

Begin in the upper right-hand corner and work from right to left. Bring the needle up from the back of the canvas through the 2nd hole down from the top outline edge of the piece. Leave an inch or so of wool at the back to be locked in by the first few stitches. Insert the needle in the 2nd hole up 1 row to the right and bring it out through the hole directly to the left of where the 1st stitch began (diagram 1). Continue in this manner across the canvas. To finish a row, leave the needle at the back of the canvas, inserted in the top row.

To do *the 2nd row*, invert the canvas, and bring the needle to the front through the hole directly to the left of what is now the top of your last stitch. Insert the needle in the 2nd hole up 1 row to the right, and bring it out through the hole directly to the left of where the 1st stitch in the 2nd row began (diagram 2). Continue back across the canvas. At the end of the row, leave the needle at the back of the canvas, inserted in the top row.

(1)

To do *the 3rd row*, invert the canvas, and bring the needle back to the front through the 2nd hole down 1 row to the left. Insert the needle in the 2nd hole above 1 row to the right, and work back across the canvas.

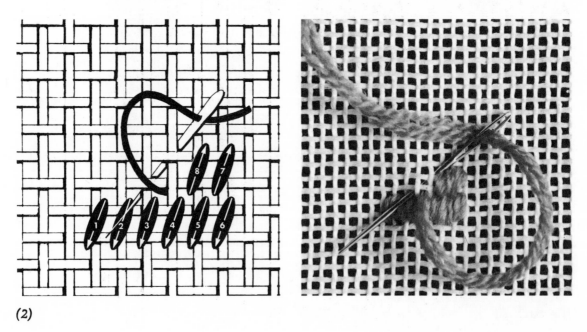

(2)

PARISIAN STITCH

This stitch is a combination of a short and a long Gobelin stitch and gives an interesting texture for background work. The full 3-ply wool or full tapestry yarn should be used and the stitches kept very relaxed, because if they are pulled too tightly the vertical threads of canvas will show through.

The Parisian stitch can be worked either from left to right or right to left, so it is not necessary to invert the canvas at the end of a row.

To make the 1st or short stitch, beginning in the upper left, bring the needle out leaving enough yarn to be locked in by the first stitches. Insert the needle in the 2nd hole directly above, and bring it out in the next row to the right, 1 hole below where the 1st stitch started.

For the 2nd or long stitch, skip 3 holes, and insert the needle in the 4th hole directly above. Bring the needle back out in the row to the right, 3rd hole down (or 1 row above where the 2nd stitch began).

Now alternate with short and long stitches across the canvas. When you have made the last stitch (a short one), bring the needle out in the same row and through the 4th hole down from the bottom of the short stitch.

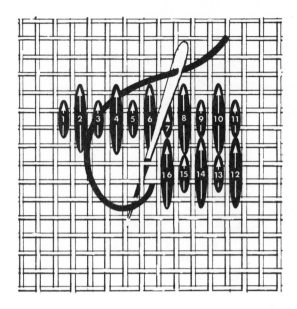

You are now ready to work the Parisian stitch from right to left. Skip 3 holes, and insert the needle in the 4th directly above. This will be the bottom hole of your last short stitch. Bring the needle out through the 2nd hole down directly beneath the long stitch in the top row. Insert the needle in the same hole as the bottom of the upper long stitch, and bring it out in the row to the left through the 3rd hole down.

Alternate the long and short stitches back across the canvas.

As with all other stitches, if you are ever in doubt about what you are doing, leave the needle at the back of the canvas and think about what you want the yarn to accomplish and how it can be done most simply! Once you have solved the problem and understand it, you will have no difficulty in learning the stitch.

MOSAIC STITCH

A good filler for backgrounds, the Mosaic stitch gives a small square effect. Use full 3-ply Persian or full tapestry yarn.

Begin in the upper right-hand corner by bringing the needle out in the 2nd row from the right edge, 3rd hole down, leaving enough yarn at the back to be locked in by the first few stitches.

The *1st stitch* is a continental stitch, which is made by inserting the needle in the next row to the right in the row above. Complete the stitch by bringing the needle to the front in the hole to the left of where the 1st stitch began.

The *2nd stitch* is made by diagonally skipping a hole and inserting the needle directly above the 1st stitch. Bring it out in the same vertical row as the 2nd stitch began, 1 hole above.

To make the *3rd stitch*, insert the needle in the row above, 1 hole to the right. Bring it out 1 row to the left of where the 2nd stitch began. These 3 slanting stitches form a square.

The needle is now in the same horizontal row as the beginning of the previous stitches. Repeat the 3-stitch square, 1 continental, 1 long diagonal, and 1 continental. Work in this manner across the area to be covered. When the last stitch of the square has been completed, leave the needle at the back of the canvas.

2nd row: Invert the canvas and bring the needle out in the 2nd hole in from the right (a hole already worked). Continue across the row. When you have completed the last stitch, leave the needle at the back of the canvas.

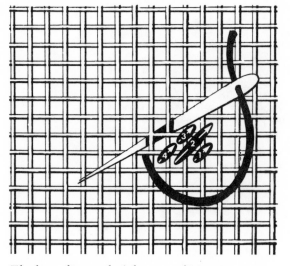

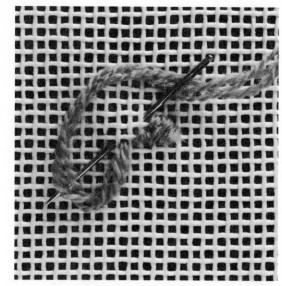

The long diagonal of the second Mosaic square

3rd row: Invert the canvas. Skip 1 horizontal row and bring the needle out in the 2nd hole in from the right edge (same vertical row as the one in which the first stitch in the row above began). Complete the row. Leave the needle at the back of the canvas.

Invert the canvas and repeat instructions for remaining rows.

SCOTCH STITCH

An interesting and effective stitch to use for backgrounds, this stitch fills in quickly and creates an extremely interesting texture.

The important thing to keep in mind is that the 5 graduating diagonal stitches form a square—3 holes vertically and 3 holes horizontally.

Scotch stitch may be done with the diagonals of the squares all going in the same direction, or you can achieve a checkerboard effect by having the diagonals go in opposite directions, as the diagram and stitch photographs show.

It may help to draw the top and right side of the 1st square on the canvas in pencil. The 1st stitched square will guide you in making the 2nd, and so on.

Use full 3-ply Persian or full tapestry yarn.

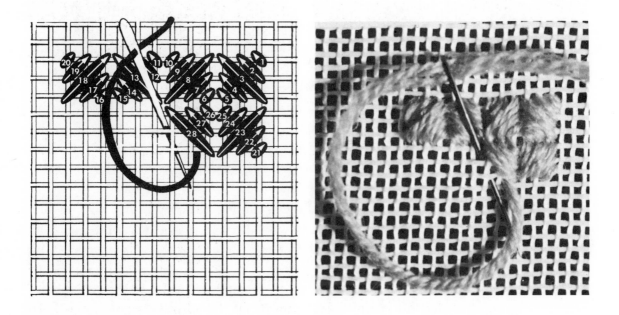

The *1st diagonal stitch* is made by bringing the needle out 1 hole down from the upper right-hand corner of the area to be filled. Leave an inch of the yarn at the back to be locked in by the first few stitches. Insert the needle in the row above and 1 square to the left. Bring it out in the square directly below where the 1st stitch started.

The *2nd diagonal stitch* is made by inserting the needle in the hole to the left of the top stitch. Bring it out directly under where the 2nd stitch started.

The *3rd and longest diagonal stitch* is made by inserting the needle in the hole directly to the left of the top of the 2nd stitch. This stitch forms the center diagonal of the Scotch-stitch square.

Bring the needle out in the square to the left of where the 3rd stitch began. Insert the needle in the square directly below the top of the 3rd stitch. Bring the needle out in the square to the left of where the 4th stitch began.

The *final stitch* is made by inserting the needle 1 row above and 1 square to the left, bringing it out in the next row to the left, 1 hole down.

You are ready to start the second Scotch-stitch square, which, as you can see from the diagram, slants in the opposite direction.

The *1st stitch* is made by inserting the needle in the row to the right, 1 hole up (in the same hole as the top of the 5th stitch of the previous square). Bring the needle out through the hole to the left of where the 1st stitch began.

For the *2nd diagonal stitch*, insert the needle in the hole directly above the top of the 1st stitch. Bring it out through the hole to the left of where the 2nd stitch began.

To make the *3rd and longest diagonal stitch*, insert the needle in the hole above the top of the 2nd stitch.

Bring the needle out directly above the beginning of the 3rd stitch and insert it in the hole to the left of the top of the 3rd or longest stitch. Bring it out in the hole above the beginning of the 4th stitch.

The *final stitch* is made by inserting the needle in the hole above and 1 row to the right, bringing it out through the same hole where the 5th stitch started.

You are now ready to repeat the first Scotch square. Continue alternating the slants of the squares across the canvas.

At the end of the row, run the yarn under the last few stitches on the back and snip it off.

To start the next row, bring the needle up in the 2nd row in from the right edge of the area to be worked, 3rd hole down. Follow directions for the second Scotch-stitch square (see above) to make the first square in this row. If you want the checkerboard effect shown in the diagram, make the slant of the stitches of each Scotch-stitch square opposite to the slant of the stitches forming the square above it as well as the one next to it.

BRICK STITCH

The brick stitch is a vertical stitch like the straight Gobelin or a bargello stitch. The size of the stitch is small, because each stitch skips only 1 hole. It has more textural interest than the tent stitch, and is practical for backgrounds or large areas.

The brick stitch can be worked on either mono or Penelope

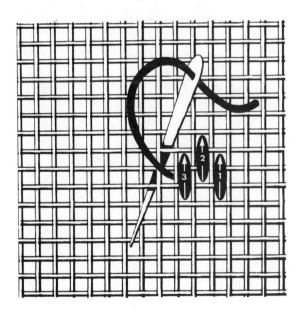

canvas. It is not recommended for use on #5 canvas because it does not cover satisfactorily. Use full 3-ply Persian or full tapestry yarn.

Starting at the right, bring the needle out through the 4th hole down from the top, leaving enough yarn at back to be locked in by the first few stitches. Skip the hole directly above and insert the needle in the next hole up bringing it out 1 row to the left, and 1 hole down.

Make the 2nd vertical stitch by skipping the hole directly above and inserting the needle in the next hole and bringing it out 1 row to the left, 3 holes down (same horizontal row as where the 1st stitch began).

Work to the end of the row in this "sawtooth" manner, then invert the canvas. Work back across the canvas in the same manner being sure to cover all the horizontal canvas threads.

On #10 (Penelope) canvas

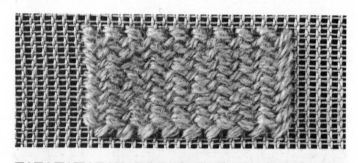

On #5 (Penelope) canvas

HERRINGBONE STITCH

The herringbone stitch is a background or border stitch. It should be worked on Penelope canvas and can only be worked on mono if you use the embroidery method, that is, moving your needle hand from the back to the front of the canvas with each stitch. It is extremely handsome on #5 canvas using rug wool, and is most effective when a different color is used in each row. It fills in rapidly and gives a wonderful woven textured effect.

Begin in the upper left-hand corner of the area to be filled. Bring the needle out through the corner hole, leaving an inch or so on the back to be locked in. Watch to be sure that the tag end gets locked in as there is very little yarn at the back of the herringbone stitch.

To make the *1st stitch*, diagonally skip a square and insert the needle in the 2nd row to the right, 2nd hole down. Bring it out in the square directly to the left in the same horizontal row.

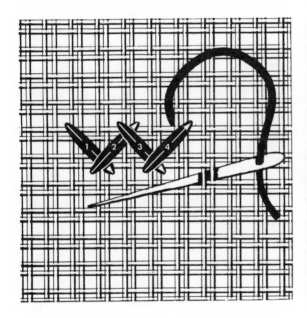 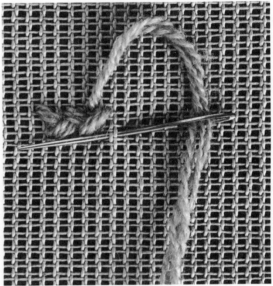

To make the *2nd stitch*, diagonally skip a square and insert the needle in the 2nd row to the right, 2nd hole up. Bring the needle out in the hole directly to the left in the same horizontal row.

The *3rd stitch* is made the same as the 1st and so on across the row.

Work from left to right (which is the only way the herringbone stitch can be done). When you are forming the bottom part of the stitch, be sure your needle comes out *under* the loose loop of yarn from your needle. When you are forming the top of a stitch, the needle should come out *over* the yarn.

To begin *the 2nd row,* start again at the left side by locking your yarn through several of the worked stitches at the back in a zigzag pattern. Repeat the same stitches as before, being careful that the top and bottom of each stitch is worked through the holes directly under the ones in the row above. Sometimes you must use your thumb or needle to move the overlapping stitch that slants from left to right in the row above in order to see where the needle should be brought out.

HUNGARIAN STITCH

Another variation to be used for a textured background is the Hungarian stitch. It is a combination of short and long vertical stitches much the same as the Parisian stitch but with a slightly less regular pattern. You can vary the color of yarn in each row. Alternating two colors gives a strong textured look. Alternating several colors results in a bargello effect.

Use full 3-ply Persian or full tapestry yarn. Beginning at the upper right-hand corner, bring the needle out 4 holes down from the top, leaving enough yarn on the back to be locked in by the next few stitches.

1st stitch: Making a vertical stitch, skip the hole directly above and insert the needle in the next hole up. Bring it out in the row to the left, 3rd hole down. This will be 1 row below where the 1st stitch started.

2nd stitch: Skip 3 holes and insert the needle in the 4th directly

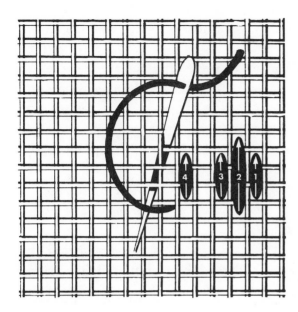 

above and bring it out 1 row to the left, 3rd hole down. This will be the same horizontal row as where the 1st stitch began.

3rd stitch: This is a short stitch that skips 1 hole and matches the 1st. You now have a long stitch in the center with matching short stitches on either side.

Skip the next vertical row to the left and then repeat the above 3 stitches using the same horizontal rows of the canvas as you used for the 1st 3. Continue in this manner across the area to be filled, skipping a vertical row between each set of 3 stitches, and ending the row with a short stitch.

If you are using the same color throughout, invert the canvas to work back across.

2nd row (when using same color): After you invert the canvas, bring the needle out through the same hole as what is now the top of the last stitch. Make a short vertical stitch skipping 1 hole. Skip the next vertical row, make a matching short stitch, and bring the needle out in the next row to the left, 3rd hole down. The next stitch is the long one, skipping 3 holes and inserting the needle in the 4th. Bring the needle out in the next row to the left, 3rd hole down, which is the same hole as the top of an already worked short stitch. Make another short stitch skipping 1 hole. Now you can see the pattern of 1 long stitch sandwiched between 2 short ones beginning to fill in the background.

Skip the next vertical row and repeat the short, long, short stitches. Work in the same manner back across the canvas ending with a short stitch. Leave needle at back of canvas.

3rd row (when using same color): Invert the canvas. Bring needle up in the last row to the right through the 2nd hole down. Continue across the canvas following directions for first row.

If the next row is to be a different color, end the 1st row by running the yarn under the finished stitches on the back and begin the second color at the right edge again.

Skip one horizontal row below the previous row and bring the needle out in the last row to the right. Make a short stitch by skipping 1 hole and inserting the needle in the next hole up, which is one already worked by the short stitch directly above.

Skip the next vertical row and make a matching short stitch. Bring the needle out in the next row to the left, 3rd hole down.

Make a long stitch skipping 3 holes and entering the 4th. Put a matching short stitch on the left.

Skip the next vertical row and repeat the 3-stitch pattern, short, long, short. Work across the canvas in this manner ending the row with a short stitch. Run the yarn under some of the stitches on the back and snip it off.

Start the new row by bringing the needle up in the last row to the right, 2nd hole down.

In all cases use the full strand of yarn, and if you are working on #10 canvas be sure to leave the yarn very relaxed so the canvas does not show through.

6

Blocking the Finished Work

A finished piece of needlepoint is almost always out of shape, either to a slight degree or to the point of complete distortion. This is caused by the tension of the wool against the canvas, which gets softer as it is handled.

If the piece is only slightly out of shape, press it on the wrong side with a steam iron or with a hot iron and a damp cloth. This steaming and pressing gives the yarn a nice finish and makes the unworked canvas margins easier to handle.

Blocking is used for canvas that needs to be stretched back into shape. The process is not really difficult but requires a few essentials, such as a piece of plywood larger than the finished piece of needlepoint, rustproof tacks—and patience! Some people tack the needlepoint to the inside of a closet door or onto a closet floor, but plywood is much handier.

Cover the plywood with wrapping paper and draw on it the original dimensions of the piece. Dampen the needlepoint with a sponge or cloth dipped in cold water until the piece is quite wet. Do not dip it in water because that makes it *too* wet.

Place the piece face down, and pull and stretch it until it conforms to the paper outline as closely as possible. Using rustproof thumbtacks, pushpins, or carpet tacks, tack one of the corners to the board. Never place the tacks near the actual needlepoint stitches. Next, tack the corner diagonally opposite, so that the shape aligns with the paper pattern. Then, tack a third corner into position.

Placing the tacks about 1 inch apart, work along the two sides between the three tacked corners, making sure the line is true. Now, tug and stretch until the remaining two sides meet the line of the pattern and finish tacking it down.

Let the piece dry completely before removing it from the blocking board. Drying may take a day or two. A spot with good air circulation will help speed drying somewhat, but heat will cause the wool to shrink, a most unpleasant prospect.

If the piece is still out of shape when it has dried, it should be blocked again. The second blocking will require less effort.

Many needlepoint shops and upholstery shops will block pieces for a fee. Professional blocking might be worth looking into for especially complex (think of all those hours of stitching!) or oversize needlepoint pieces.

$\mathcal{C} \mathcal{O}$ 7

Accessories and Gifts

An original needlepoint creation is one of the most flattering and welcome gifts to receive and most satisfying to give.

The projects that follow have been selected with an eye to their usefulness as well as to their suitability as gifts. The small pieces are quite economical: many can be worked with scraps of canvas and leftover yarn from larger projects, and most can be finished completely at home.

The instructions will help you get started. Wherever it is practical, other uses are suggested for the design specified for each project. Sometimes a design worked on #12 canvas (see Anemone Coaster, on following page) can be used for something entirely different if worked on #5 canvas. Or parts of a design (see Signal-Flag Belt, page 69) can be used for other projects. When you feel comfortable and confident in your work, you are sure to find many ways of applying what you have learned to your own creative ideas.

ANEMONE COASTER
Color photograph following page 104.

A needlepoint coaster that harmonizes with the decor of a room is both a useful safeguard for fine furniture and a colorful accessory. Placed where guests might conveniently rest their drinks, it will brighten the scene and avoid rings on your table as well. A set of four coasters is a charming and inexpensive gift and can be made from scraps of canvas and leftover wool.

This same design, worked in rug wool on #5 canvas, would make an attractive 10-inch x 10-inch pillow cover. On #10 canvas, the size of the finished piece would be slightly larger than the coaster—about 5 inches square—a good size for a small hot pad. Choose your own colors for this, or use the colors suggested below.

Materials Needed

Size of finished coaster is approximately 4¾ inches square.
Quantities of wool specified below are for 3-ply Persian wool. (Equivalent in tapestry yarn: 1 strand Persian wool equals 30 inches.)

> #12 canvas, 9 inches x 9 inches
> #18 needle
> 8 strands red wool (Color A)
> 4 strands green wool (Color B)
> 8 strands yellow wool (Color C)
> 16 strands blue wool (Color D)
> 8 strands turquoise wool (Color E)
> 8 strands light blue wool (Color F)
> 2 strands black wool (Color G)
> 2 strands white wool (Color H)
> 1 piece felt (5 inches x 5 inches) for backing
> All-purpose glue

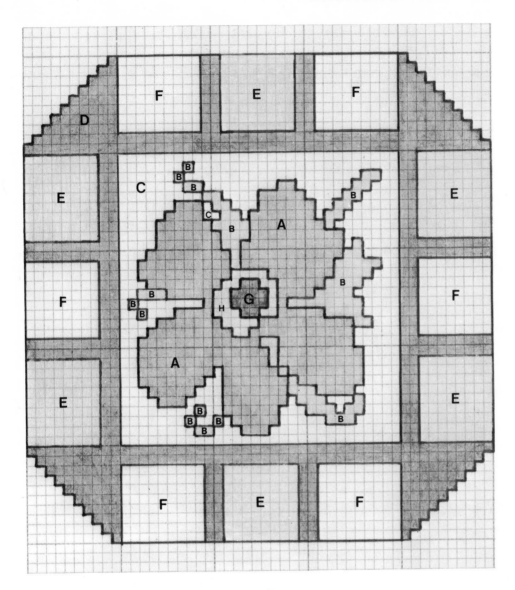

Instructions

Bind the edges of the canvas with masking or adhesive tape. Mark the outline of the coaster in the center of the canvas.

Follow the chart to fill in the pattern, or to mark the pattern on canvas. (See page 13.) This design is worked with 2 plys of Persian wool or full tapestry yarn. Use the basket-weave or continental method. Basket weave fills in quickly and you will not need to invert the canvas after completing each row.

Finishing

When the needlepoint is complete, press it on the wrong side with a steam iron or a hot iron and a damp cloth. (Unless it is badly out of shape, a small piece rarely needs to be blocked.)

Trim the unworked margins to ½ inch all around. Snip the corners, fold the margins under, and press flat. Cut a piece of felt the same size as the coaster, and glue it to the needlepoint. Place the coaster on a flat surface (stitched side up), and put a weight on it until the glue is thoroughly dry. Two or three heavy books will provide the necessary weight.

FLAME-STITCH EYEGLASS CASE
Color photograph following page 104.

Flame-stitch patterns are effective and can be worked quickly. They are used on pillows, purses, tote bags, belts, bench and chair seats, as well as eyeglass cases.

The eyeglass case is a fine project for a beginner; it is small, easy to work, and affords a good opportunity to learn and practice this versatile stitch.

Materials Needed

Size of finished eyeglass case is approximately 3¾ inches x 6½ inches.

Quantities of wool specified below are for 3-ply Persian wool. (Equivalent in tapestry yarn: 1 ounce Persian wool equals 40 yards.)

> #14 canvas, 8 inches x 11 inches
> #19 needle
> ½ ounce each of three colors of wool (A, B, C)
> 2 pieces (each about 5 inches x 10 inches) buckram for interlining
> 2 pieces (each about 5 inches x 10 inches) silk or faille (or similar fabric) for lining
> All-purpose glue
> 1 piece (about 5 inches x 10 inches) light felt, suede cloth, or similar fabric for back of case
> Lining and backing fabrics should be chosen to match, harmonize, or look well with, the yarn colors used in the needlepoint design.

Note: *The materials listed above are for an eyeglass case made with needlepoint front and fabric or felt back. If you want to make both front and back in needlepoint—which is even more attractive—double the quantities of wool and omit buckram and backing fabric. Only lining is needed.*

Instructions

Bind the edges of the canvas with masking or adhesive tape. Mark the outline of the area to be worked in the center of the canvas. Work with full 3-ply yarn.

With Color A, begin at the lowest point of the V at the center of the long side, as indicated by X on the chart. (See note on how to follow chart for Flame-stitch design on page 38.) To make the 1st stitch, bring the needle from back to front, leaving about an inch of yarn to be worked in by the first few stitches. The stitch is made absolutely vertically, skipping 3 holes, and entering the 4th (4 horizontal threads are now covered, corresponding to the 4 squares shown on chart). Remember to leave the wool relaxed. Bring the needle back through the canvas in the next row to the left, 2nd hole down. (See note on counting holes on page 35.)

Working upward, skip 3 holes and enter the 4th, bringing the needle out in the next row to the left through the 2nd hole down. Repeat upward for another single stitch. You now have 3 single stitches sidestepping upward. Bring the needle out through the 2nd hole down in the next row to the left.

The next 2 stitches are made exactly the same, except that they are right next to each other instead of stepped up. This is a double stitch. Next bring the needle out through the 2nd hole down in the next row to the left. Skip 3 holes up, entering the 4th, and repeat this same stitch 3 times more without stepping up but moving 1 row to the left with each stitch. Bring the needle out through the 2nd hole down in the next row to the left. Then do 4 stitches next to each other without stepping up.

Now it is time to decrease. Starting 2 holes down in the row to the left, do 3 stitches next to each other without stepping up. Starting 2 holes down in the row to the left, do 2 stitches next to each other; and then, 2 holes down, 1 row to the left, start doing the 3 single stitches sidestepping up each time. The 3rd single stitch is the peak of the flame.

Invert the canvas and repeat the same pattern, but now work upward from left to right. Two more single sidestepping stitches, 2 stitches next to each other, 3 stitches next to each other, 4 next to each other. Then decrease: 3 next to each other, 2 next to each other and then the single ones as shown on the chart. At the peak of the flame, invert the canvas and continue the design until you reach the edge of the piece as shown on the graph. When you come to the edge of the piece, run the yarn through 5 or 6 worked stitches on the back and snip it off.

Invert the piece so that your 1st stitch is again at the bottom. With Color A run the yarn under 5 or 6 worked stitches on the back, so that you can bring it out in the next line to the right of the 1st stitch, through the 2nd hole up (Y on chart). Then stitch upward to the right using the same pattern as before. Glance to the left side of the piece now and again; the 2 stitches next to each other should be on the same horizontal line as the previous 2, and so on up the line to the top single one. If they do not align, something is wrong. Find the mistake and correct it.

When you reach the peak of the flame, invert the canvas, and work upward from right to left. Continue the design until you reach the edge of the piece, as shown on the graph. Run the yarn through stitches on the back, and snip it off.

The pattern is now set up, and you simply follow it to fill in the rest of the piece. Remember to invert the canvas each time you reach the peak of a flame.

Starting with Color B, begin at the right edge by locking in the end of yarn through the worked stitches on the back. Bring the wool out to the front (at Z, as shown on the chart), and start working upward to the left. The bottom of each stitch should come through to the front in the same hole as the top stitch of the preceding zigzag line. All horizontal threads of the canvas must be covered.

Finishing

After the completed needlepoint for the eyeglass case has been pressed or blocked (see page 55), trim the canvas around the edge of the stitched area, leaving a ½-inch margin of unworked canvas. Turn the canvas margins to the back, and stitch by hand to the back of the needlepoint. The pressing or blocking will have made the canvas soft and easy to manage.

Cut two pieces of buckram slightly smaller than the eyeglass case outline. Cut two pieces of the lining material about ¼ inch larger than the buckram all the way around. With all-purpose glue, secure the lining fabric to the buckram, turning the ¼-inch margin over the edge of the buckram and gluing it down. (Cut ⅛-inch slashes in the curved area to make it easier to turn edge.)

Cut the backing fabric to the shape of the eyeglass case, adding ½-inch margin all around. Fold the margin under (a few slashes in the curved area will make it fold under more easily), and press it with a steam iron.

Place the two silk sides of the buckram pieces face to face. Sandwich them between the needlepoint and the backing. Stitch the case together on three sides, using tiny stitches as close to the edge as possible. Leave one short end open. At the open end, the needlepoint and the backing can be fastened to the lining either by stitching or gluing. If you sew them together, catch a few threads of needlepoint (or backing) and a few threads of lining, keeping the stitches small and close to the inner edges of both pieces. The joining should be almost invisible. A light glue application near the open edges, followed (when the glue is absolutely dry) by careful stitching, would give an even more secure finish.

MOTTO PINCUSHION
Color photograph following page 104.

A pincushion is an inexpensive gift that can be made quickly. Only a small piece of canvas is needed, and this is a good way to use up leftover wool.

The motto used in the pincushion in the color photograph is "Stick pins in me." You will find other suggested mottoes on page 124 and alternate alphabets on pages 126 and 127.

Materials Needed

Size of finished pincushion is approximately 5⅓ inches x 7 inches.

Quantities of wool specified below are for 3-ply Persian wool. (Equivalent in tapestry yarn: 1 ounce Persian wool equals 40 yards; 1 strand equals 30 inches.)

> #10 canvas, 11 inches x 13 inches
> #17 needle
> 14 strands of green wool (Color A)
> 10 strands of pink wool (Color B)
> 15 strands of blue wool (Color C)
> 1 ounce of white wool (Color D)
> ½ yard muslin
> Pillow stuffing (Dacron® polyester fiberfill, shredded foam, strips of old nylon stockings, pine needles, or cotton puffs all make good fillers.)
> 1 piece (about 7 inches x 9 inches) fabric for backing (velvet, felt, moire, faille, silk are suggested)

Instructions

Bind the edges of the canvas with masking or adhesive tape.

Mark the outline of the area to be worked in the center of the canvas. Then transfer the border and lettering from the chart (on facing page) to the canvas with a waterproof marker or with a small brush and acrylic paint thinned with water. Each filled-in square on

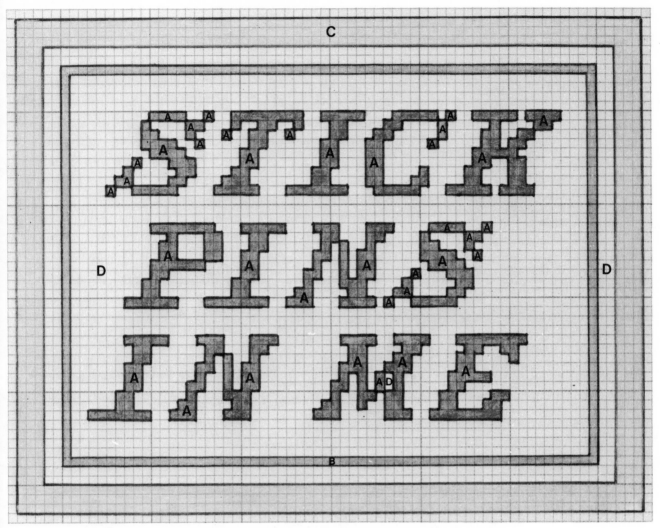

The lettering is worked in Color A, the inner border in Color B, the outer border in Color C, and the background in Color D.

the chart represents a stitch. The top right stitch of the S is worked over the intersection of the 11th thread down from the top edge of the outline and the 22nd thread from the left edge. Once this position has been established, you can easily mark the position of the rest of the lettering. It is simply a matter of counting.

The lettering should be filled in last since the background is in white.

Use the full 3-ply wool. Following the chart, begin the 3 rows of colored edging in the upper right-hand corner using either the continental or basket-weave method. The next 2 rows of background color framing the piece can be done with either method. The single line of framing color must be done with the continental method. The background can then be filled in with either the continental or basket-weave method, leaving the marked lettering unworked.

When the background is completed, work the lettering with the continental method.

Finishing

To make a pincushion form, cut two pieces of muslin ¼ inch larger than the finished needlepoint. (This allows ½ inch for seam allowance.) Sew the pieces together on three sides and turn right side out. Stuff firmly with the filler you prefer. Fold edges of the open end in and stitch closed.

After the needlepoint has been pressed or blocked (see page 55), trim the canvas around the worked area allowing a ½-inch margin all around. Place needlepoint and backing fabric right sides together. Stitch around three sides. Turn right side out. Insert the stuffed pincushion form. Turn in edges of the open end of the needlepoint piece, and stitch closed with tiny invisible stitches.

SIGNAL-FLAG BELT
Color photograph following page 104.

A needlepoint belt is bound to be a conversation piece! A belt lettered with a motto, such as "Every day in every way I grow thinner," would be an amusing gift to give to a diet-conscious friend. Belts made with nautical signal flags can spell out a message or a name, or simply add a salty touch to a sailing costume. The separate signal-flag designs would also make appealing coasters or cushions for a boating enthusiast. A combination of any two would turn an inexpensive wallet into an elegant accessory.

Materials Needed

Size of belt with 15 flags as given is approximately 2 inches x 30 inches.

Quantities of wool specified below are for 3-ply Persian wool. (Equivalent in tapestry yarn: 1 ounce Persian wool equals 40 yards; 1 strand equals 30 inches.)

> #10 canvas, 6 inches x 38 inches (length depending on waist size)
> #17 needle
> 2 ounces red wool (Color A)
> 1 ounce white wool (Color B)
> 2 ounces blue wool (Color C)
> ½ ounce yellow wool (Color D)
> 4 strands black wool (Color E)
> 1 yard felt or thin leather (or sturdy fabric such as canvas or upholstery-weight linen), about 3 inches wide, for backing
> A grommet die*
> 4 brass grommets
> Brass buckle

Many upholstery shops or craft supply houses sell grommet dies and grommets. Request ½-inch brass grommets.

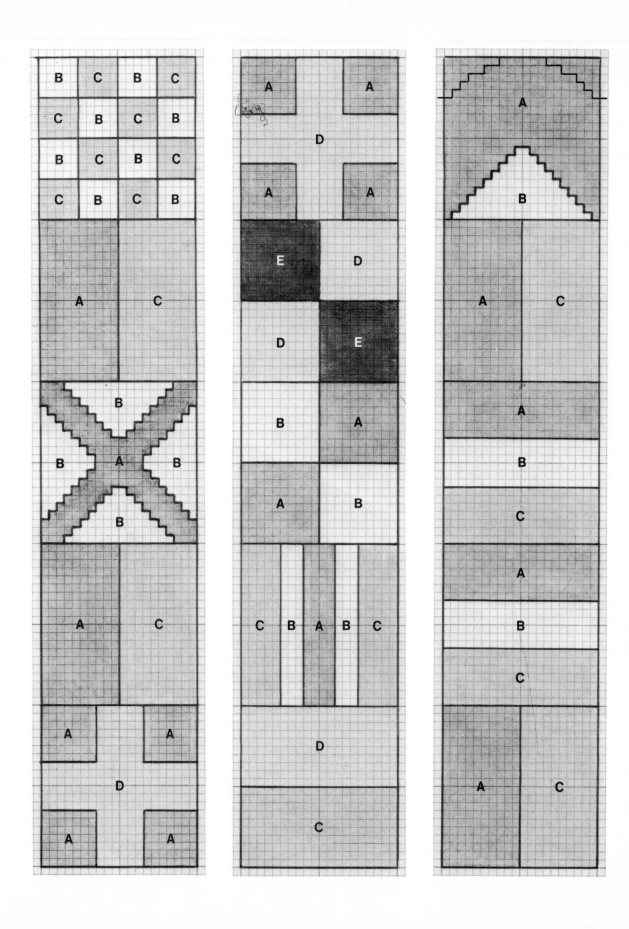

Instructions

Bind the edges of the canvas with masking or adhesive tape. Mark the area to be worked in the center of the canvas. (A belt 30 inches long will fit a 26-inch waist. Check size of waist and alternate finishing instructions on page 73, then adjust the length as necessary.) Each signal flag is 2 inches wide.

On page 72 you will find drawings of all the signal flags with the letters they represent. If you want to arrange the flags to spell out a particular name or message, it is best to plot them on graph paper first to be sure that placement and spacing will work out. (See page 14.) The flags can be made square or oblong to fit your needs.

Use the full 3-ply Persian or full tapestry yarn. Work the design in basket-weave method so it will not be necessary to invert the canvas after completing each row.

Finishing

When the belt has been completed and the piece has been pressed or blocked (see page 55), trim the unworked canvas, allowing a ½-inch margin all around. Fold the margin back, and stitch by hand to the back of the needlepoint.

Cut a piece of backing fabric or thin leather the width and 2 inches shorter than the needlepoint belt, allowing ½-inch seam all around. (If felt is used, no seam allowance is necessary.)

To fasten the buckle to the end of the belt, cut another piece of backing fabric the width of the belt and 4 inches long, plus ½-inch seam allowance all around. Turn under seam allowance. With right sides facing up, lap one short end of this tab over the buckle end of the needlepoint, and machine-stitch in place.

Fold the tab back over the end of the belt ½ inch from the stitching. Punch a hole in the center of this fold line, and insert the prong of the buckle. Fold the tab back, and pin it to the wrong side of the needlepoint. Make a row of stitches across the tab as close to the buckle as possible.

Although the chart on the facing page is divided into three parts, the belt is worked in one piece. To make the rounded end that goes through the buckle, follow the stairstep outline indicated at the top of the section at the right.

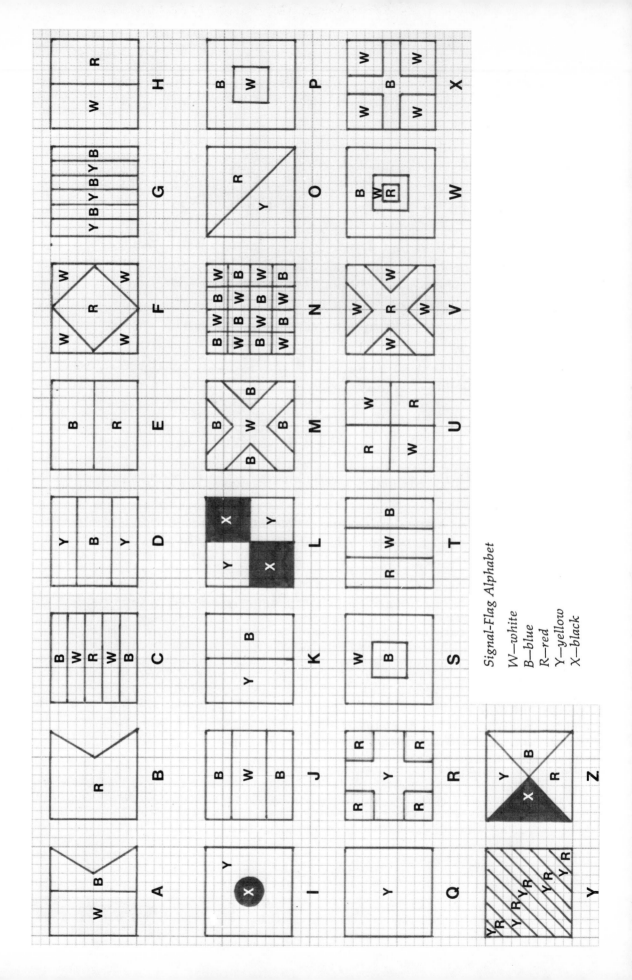

Signal-Flag Alphabet

W—white
B—blue
R—red
Y—yellow
X—black

Cut a third strip from the backing fabric or thin leather 1 inch wide and 5 inches long. Turn under ¼-inch seam allowances on the two long sides and machine-stitch. Loop strip loosely around belt about 2 inches from the buckle, and secure ends on wrong side of needlepoint. (If felt is used, cut a strip ½ inch wide and 5 inches long; loop around belt and secure ends.)

Now turn under the seam allowance all around the longer piece of backing fabric or leather. (Felt backing is sewn to needlepoint without turning edges under.) Pin to back of belt, lapping one end over the end of the buckle tab and matching the other edges all around. Machine-stitch to belt.

At the end opposite the buckle, punch four holes through the needlepoint and backing with a sharp object. The first should be 3½ inches from the end, and the holes should be spaced at 1-inch intervals. The holes should be about the circumference of a lead pencil. Place the lower part of a brass grommet on the grommet die. Place one of the holes on the grommet die (over the lower part of the brass grommet), then the top part of the grommet and the top of the grommet die on top of that. Strike with a hammer to seal the grommet. Repeat on the other holes.

If you would like an easier way to finish a belt, try this:

Work the needlepoint strip long enough to overlap 6 inches. When it is completed and blocked, trim the unworked canvas, allowing a ½-inch margin all around. Fold the margin back, and stitch it by hand to the back of the needlepoint. Cut a piece of lining fabric the width and length of the belt, allowing a ½-inch margin all around. Turn in the margins, and stitch the lining to the back of the needlepoint. (If you use felt for the backing, cut it the same width as the needlepoint, and stitch or glue it to the back of the piece.) Use a horse-blanket pin or large safety pin to fasten the belt instead of a buckle.

Another simple way to fasten the belt is with felt ties. Make the needlepoint piece 2 inches shorter than waist measure. Cut two strips of heavy felt ½ inch to ¾ inches wide and 18 inches long. Machine-stitch a strip to the center of each end of the needlepoint piece before backing is attached.

INITIALED BOOKMARK
Color photograph following page 104.

The Greek key design used here is based on the continuing repeat system and can be made in different lengths, depending upon the number of times the motif is repeated. The same design worked on #5 or #3 mesh canvas would make an interesting rug border. Worked on #10 mesh, it could be used for luggage rack straps. For the bookmark, which is made on #12 mesh, the design ends with an initial from the lettering chart on page 127.

Materials Needed

Size of finished bookmark is approximately 1¾ inches x 12 inches.

Quantities of wool specified below are for 3-ply Persian wool. (Equivalent in tapestry yarn: 1 ounce Persian wool equals 40 yards.)

>   #12 canvas, 6 inches x 16 inches
>   #18 needle
>   ½ ounce green wool (Color A)
>   ½ ounce orange wool (Color B)
>   1 piece of felt (about 2 inches x 12½ inches) for backing
>   All-purpose glue

Instructions

Bind the canvas edges with masking or adhesive tape. Mark the outline of the area to be worked in the center of the canvas. Work with 2 plys of Persian wool or full-ply tapestry yarn.

Begin in the upper right-hand corner about an inch down and an inch in from the edge. Follow the chart. Either the continental or basket-weave method may be used. The broken part of the Greek key design (part worked in orange in bookmark photographed), which also forms the border, should be worked first. The line is 2 stitches wide and follows the pattern on the chart, each square representing a stitch.

When you have completed the design, find the initial you want (on page 127) and transfer it to the canvas in the position indicated on the chart. Use the continental method to work the initial (in the same color as the Greek key design).

Then fill in the background.

Finishing

When the needlepoint is finished, press it on the wrong side with a damp cloth and hot iron. (A piece as small as this rarely needs blocking.) Trim the unworked canvas to leave a margin of ½ inch all around. Snip the corners, fold back the margin, and press it down. Cut a piece of felt the same size, and glue it to the back of the needlepoint. Place the finished bookmark, right side up, under a weight, and allow glue to dry completely.

MONOGRAMMED NAPKIN RING
Color photograph following page 104.

If there is a lady on your gift list who "has everything," monogrammed napkin rings in needlepoint are the answer to your problem. They are easy and fun to make. The same pattern can be used to make an attractive "dog collar" choker.

Materials Needed

Size of finished napkin ring is approximately 2 inches x 7 inches.

Quantities of wool specified below are for 3-ply Persian wool. (Equivalent in tapestry yarn: 1 ounce Persian wool equals 40 yards; 1 strand equals 30 inches.)

 #14 canvas, 6 inches x 11 inches

 #19 needle

 ½ ounce wool of background color

 10 strands wool of monogram and trim color

 Cotton or linen fabric for backing (about 3 inches x 8 inches)

 1 yard of narrow ribbon

Instructions

Choose initials from the lettering chart on **page 78.** You will find numbers there, too. If you are giving the gift for a special occasion, you may want to include the date. A little geometric motif may be used as a filler to complete the design of the monogram, if you think it would make it more attractive. A stylized circle worked in gold wool would be appropriate if the napkin rings are being given as a wedding or anniversary present.

Lay out the monogram (and numbers and design filler, if you want to include them) on graph paper, working from the lettering charts. Check to see if the spacing looks right. The monogram should be centered.

Bind the edges of the canvas with masking or adhesive tape. Work with 2 plys of Persian wool.

ABCDEFGHIJKLM

NOPQRSTUVWX
YZ 1234567890

Following the chart, first work the initials of the monogram (and design filler) in the center of the canvas. (If you are including numbers, work them next.) The monogram (and numbers) can be worked in whichever direction is easiest—right to left, up and down. Then work the single-line outline of the monogram. The finished width of the napkin ring should be 2 inches, and the length 7 inches. Mark the outline of the finished dimensions on the canvas.

Fill in the rest of the design with either continental or basket-weave stitches, beginning in the upper right-hand corner. The single lines would, of course, have to be done in the continental method because they go straight across.

Finishing

When the needlepoint is finished, press it on the wrong side with a steam iron or a hot iron and a damp cloth. (It is rarely necessary to block a piece as small as this.)

Cut off the taped edges, leaving about a ¾-inch canvas margin. Notch the corners if necessary. Fold these margins under, and stitch them by hand to the back of the needlepoint.

Cut a piece of cotton or linen fabric for the backing, allowing a ½-inch seam allowance all around. Fold the seam allowance under, and press.

Take a piece of contrasting or matching ribbon ¼ inch wide and 24 inches long, and either machine- or hand-stitch it lengthwise to the center of the backing. Leave 8½ inches of the ribbon free at each end to use as ties.

Stitch the backing to the needlepoint, covering the ribbon that has been sewn down. Make stitches small, close to the edge, and as invisible as possible.

BARGELLO CLUTCH BAG
Color photograph following page 104.

This classic bargello design can be adapted to make an allover pattern on a pillow cover, or it may be repeated for a belt or bellpull. The instructions below are for a small clutch bag that is not only a useful gift but offers a marvelous opportunity to use up odd bits of wool that you (or your friends) may have left over from other projects. If you prefer to use #12 canvas, instead of #14, the finished purse will be slightly larger.

Materials Needed

Size of finished Bargello Clutch Bag is approximately 3½ inches x 4½ inches.

Quantities of wool specified below are for 3-ply Persian wool. (Equivalent in tapestry yarn: 1 strand Persian wool equals 30 inches.)

> #14 canvas, 8 inches x 16 inches (for #12 canvas, 10 inches x 18 inches)
> #19 needle
> 5 strands of light orange wool (Color A)
> 6 strands of gold wool (Color B)
> 8 strands of yellow wool (Color C)
> 18 strands of lime green wool (Color D)
> 18 strands of mint green wool (Color E)
> 20 strands of kelly green wool (Color F)
> 18 strands of medium blue wool (Color G)
> 16 strands of dark blue wool (Color H)
> 14 strands of light blue wool (Color I)
> 8 strands of red wool (Color J)
> 4 strands of orange wool (Color K)
> 12 strands of fuchsia wool (Color L)
> 4 strands of lavender wool (Color M)
> ½ yard silk or other lightweight material for lining in color to harmonize with colors of wool

Instructions

Bind the edges of the canvas with masking or adhesive tape. Mark the outline of the working area on the center of the canvas. Use the full 3-ply Persian wool or full tapestry yarn.

Fold the canvas vertically and horizontally to locate the center. Follow the color key on the chart. Begin the *1st stitch* approximately 3 rows to the right of center and bring the needle out approximately 2 holes down from the center (X on chart), leaving enough yarn at the back to be locked in by the first few stitches. The stitch is vertical, skipping 3 holes and entering the 4th hole up. Bring the needle back through the canvas in the next row to the left, 2nd hole down from the top of the 1st stitch.

2nd and 3rd stitches: Skip 3 holes and enter the 4th hole above. Bring the needle out in the row to the left, 2nd hole down. Repeat. (This is called side stepping up.)

When the 3rd stitch is completed, with the needle at the front of the canvas through the 2nd hole down (from the top of the 3rd stitch), invert the canvas.

4th stitch: Insert the needle in the 4th hole directly above, and bring it out in the next row to the right, 2nd hole down.

5th stitch: Insert the needle in the 4th hole directly above, and bring it out in the next row to the *left*, 2nd hole down (a hole already worked).

6th stitch: Insert the needle in the 4th hole above, and bring it out in the next row to the left, 2nd hole down.

7th stitch: Invert the canvas, and insert the needle in the 4th hole above (a hole already worked), then bring it out in the next row to the right, 2nd hole down (a hole already worked).

8th stitch: Invert the canvas. Insert the needle in the 4th hole directly above and bring it out in the row to the right, 2nd hole down (a hole already worked).

9th stitch: Insert the needle in the 4th hole directly above. This completes a diamond of the center color.

Run the needle under some of the worked stitches on the back to lock the yarn in, and snip it off.

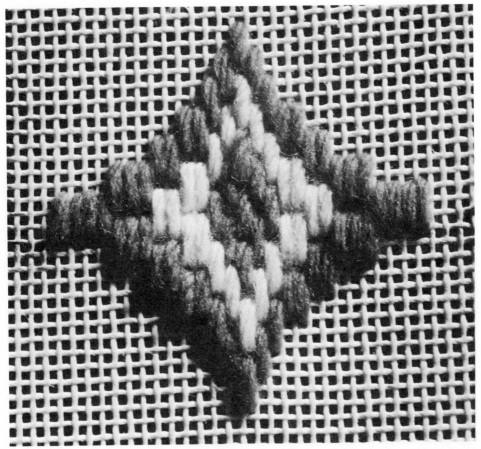

Detail of the central motif of the bargello design shown in the chart on page 81.

To start the second color, run the yarn under the worked stitches on the back, and bring the needle out through the hole already filled by the top of the 9th stitch.

Insert the needle in the 4th hole directly above (skipping 3 holes), and bring the needle out in the row to the right, 2nd hole down.

Invert the canvas and take 3 side-stepping stitches up to the left. On the 3rd stitch, bring the needle to the front of the canvas in the row to the left of where the 3rd stitch began. Skip 3 holes and enter the 4th directly above. You have made two identical stitches side by side.

Bring the needle out in the row to the left, 2 holes down. Make another vertical stitch, skipping 3 holes and entering the 4th. Bring the needle out in the row to the left of where the last stitch began, leaving the needle at the back of the canvas. You have made two identical stitches side by side.

Now, bring the needle to the front through the 2nd row to the right, 2nd hole down. This mesh has already been worked by a stitch. Make a vertical stitch, skipping 3 holes and entering the 4th. Bring the needle out in the row to the right in the 4th hole down, which has also been worked by a former stitch. Make another vertical stitch, bringing the needle out in the row to the right, 2nd hole down. Then make 3 more vertical stitches, side stepping up to the right. Now you are at the opposite point of the diamond.

Bring the needle out in the row to the right, 2nd hole down, and invert the canvas. Make 3 vertical stitches side stepping up to the left, and with the last one bring the needle out to the left through the 4th hole down. Make another identical stitch alongside it, bringing the needle out in the row to the left, 2nd hole down. Make two identical stitches on this level, leaving the needle at the back of the canvas.

Bring the needle out in the 2nd row to the right, 2nd hole down (a hole already worked), and follow the pattern back to the point of the diamond. Run the yarn under worked stitches on the back, and snip it off.

You have now formed the center motif and can add the other colors, using the same vertical stitch each time and following the chart for the number of stitches.

Remember, on the chart each stitch is indicated by 4 squares, which are actually the four threads covered. To make the stitch, the needle must come up through the hole below and go back into the canvas in the hole above the 3 skipped holes.

Finishing

When the piece is finished, press it on the wrong side with a steam iron or use a hot iron and a damp pressing cloth. (Bargello stitch rarely pulls the canvas out of shape enough to require blocking.) Trim the unworked canvas, leaving a ½-inch margin all around. Notch out the corners, fold the margin back, and stitch it by hand to the needlepoint.

Cut a piece of lining material the size of the needlepoint plus a ½-inch seam allowance all around. Fold the seam allowance under, and sew the lining to the needlepoint with small invisible stitches.

Machine-stitch a line across the width of the piece at the outer edges of the center medallion. Fold one end up, and stitch the sides together to form the pouch. (Make small stitches close to the edge so that they do not show on the outside.) The opposite end forms the envelope foldover.

MUSHROOM DOORSTOP
Color photograph following page 104.

To make an attractive and serviceable doorstop or bookend, cover a brick with needlepoint. Designs can run the gamut, but it is pleasant to personalize the design you choose if it is to be a gift. You might select a design that identifies with the person's hobbies or special collections, or use an initial or monogram so that the person receiving it knows it was made especially for him. Another thoughtful gesture is to make the piece in colors that complement the color scheme of the room in which it will be used.

The doorstop illustrated here is covered with a pattern of stylized mushrooms.

Materials Needed

Size of finished doorstop is approximately 4 inches wide x 8 inches long x 2½ inches high.

Quantities of wool specified below are for 3-ply Persian wool. (Equivalent in tapestry yarn: 1 ounce Persian wool equals 40 yards; 1 strand equals 30 inches.)

> #12 canvas, 15 inches x 20 inches
> #18 needle
> ½ ounce yellow ochre wool (Color A)
> ½ ounce lemon yellow wool (Color B)
> ½ ounce white wool (Color C)
> ½ ounce gray wool (Color D)
> 7 strands orange wool (Color E)
> 1 strand vermilion wool (Color F)
> 1½ ounces dark brown wool (Color G)
> 1 piece of felt (about 4¼ inches x 8¼ inches) to cover the bottom. (If fabric is used, add ½ inch for seam allowance.)
> 1 building brick (approximately 4 inches x 8 inches x 2½ inches)
> All-purpose glue

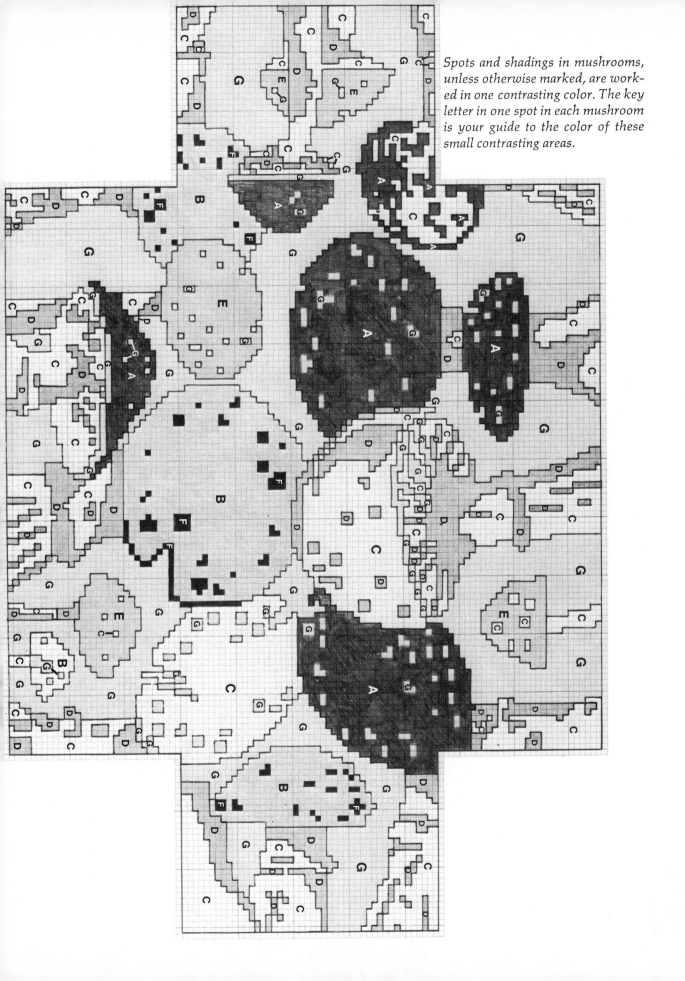

Spots and shadings in mushrooms, unless otherwise marked, are worked in one contrasting color. The key letter in one spot in each mushroom is your guide to the color of these small contrasting areas.

Instructions

Place the brick wide side down on a piece of wrapping paper, and draw around it. Next, turn the brick up on one edge and outline it. Roll the brick on the other edge and outline it, then tilt it up to trace each end. This outline gives you the pattern for the shape of the piece that will fit the brick when the cut-out corners of the rectangle are sewed up. Wrap the paper around the brick to make sure you have allowed enough ease to fit entirely around it.

Bind the edges of the canvas with masking or adhesive tape. Cut out the pattern, place it at the center of your canvas, and mark the outline on the canvas. Canvas threads are not always exactly vertical and horizontal, so your outline should follow a thread rather than the outline of the pattern.

Follow the design chart, counting each square as a stitch. You can use either the basket-weave or continental method, or a combination of both. (See page 20 for tip on finishing off wool when working a design in which there are several small areas of one color.) You may find it easier to work the dark brown background first, then the mushrooms.

Finishing

When the needlepoint is finished and blocked (see page 55), trim the canvas around the worked pattern, allowing a ½-inch margin all around.

Working with the piece inside out, sew up the corners, forming a slipcover for the brick. Turn it right side out, and insert the brick. Glue the canvas margins to the bottom of the brick on all sides.

To cover the bottom, cut a piece of felt the same size as the bottom of the brick, and glue it firmly in place.

If you use sturdy cloth for the bottom (instead of felt), cut the piece ½ inch larger than the bottom of the brick all around. Turn the ½-inch allowance under, and stitch it to the wrong side of the material. Make the needlepoint cover for the brick as described above. Insert the brick. Sew the bottom edges of the needlepoint to the edges of the bottom piece on all four sides. Stitches should be small, close to the edge, and as invisible as possible.

GEOMETRIC BOOK COVER
Color photograph following page 104.

This needlepoint book cover is designed to slip over a book that is kept nearby and used often: a television program guide, address book, or telephone book. You can choose colors to harmonize with the decoration of the room in which the book is used, or try the colors suggested below.

The project described here is sized for the cover of a television program guide (about 6 inches x 8½ inches), but it can be enlarged to fit a telephone book.

If you want to make a rug using this geometric design, use #5 or #3 mesh canvas with rug yarn.

Materials Needed

Size of finished book cover (unfolded) is approximately 8½ inches x 12½ inches.

Quantities of wool specified below are for 3-ply Persian wool. (Equivalent in tapestry yarn: 1 ounce Persian wool equals 40 yards.)

> #10 canvas, 14 inches x 18 inches
> #17 needle
> 1½ ounces black wool (for outline)
> 2½ ounces yellow wool (Color A)
> 2½ ounces red wool (Color B)
> 1 ounce white wool (Color C)
> 1 piece of heavy cardboard (8½ inches x 12½ inches)
> 1 piece of felt (8¾ inches x 12¾ inches) for lining
> 1 yard 1½-inch grosgrain ribbon
> All-purpose glue

Instructions

Bind the edges of the canvas with masking or adhesive tape. Mark the outline of the area to be worked in the center of the canvas.

Use the full 3-ply Persian wool or full tapestry yarn.

Fill in the black outline of the design first, beginning in the upper right-hand corner, as shown on the chart. Bring the needle to the front through the 19th hole over in the top line from the right edge of your outline (X on chart). Leave an inch of yarn on the back to be worked under by the first few stitches.

Work a diagonal line slanting down to the right as follows: Insert the needle 1 square up to the right and bring it out through the 2nd hole directly below. You have skipped 1 hole. Insert the needle 1 square up to the right, and bring it out through the 2nd hole down directly below. Continue this diagonal row of 19 slanting stitches to the edge of your outline. When you make the last stitch, leave the needle at the back of the canvas and fasten off.

Now the design outline continues, slanting down to the left. Bring the needle out 1 square below and to the left of where your 1st stitch began (Y on chart). Insert it upper right and bring it out 1 square below and to the left of where that stitch began. Repeat this solid line of stitches for 10 stitches, as shown on the design chart. As you can see, when a single line of stitches slants downward from right to left, it makes a solid line of stitches. When a single line slants downward from left to right, it makes a broken line of stitches.

When you have completed the black outline design, make sure there are no fuzzy tag ends of black yarn left on the back. Snip them all off so that they will not get worked into the other colors.

Fill in the yellow, red, and white as shown on the chart.

Finishing

Block the needlepoint according to the blocking instructions on page 55. Make sure the piece is a perfect rectangle, or the book cover may warp out of shape later.

Measure the finished needlepoint, and cut a piece of mat board (or cardboard) the same shape but 1/8 inch smaller all around than the needlepoint. Measure the thickness of the book to be covered, and remove a strip that wide plus 1/4 inch from the center of the board. This gap will be the spine of the book cover. The dimension of the spine for a television program guide is about 3/4 inch.

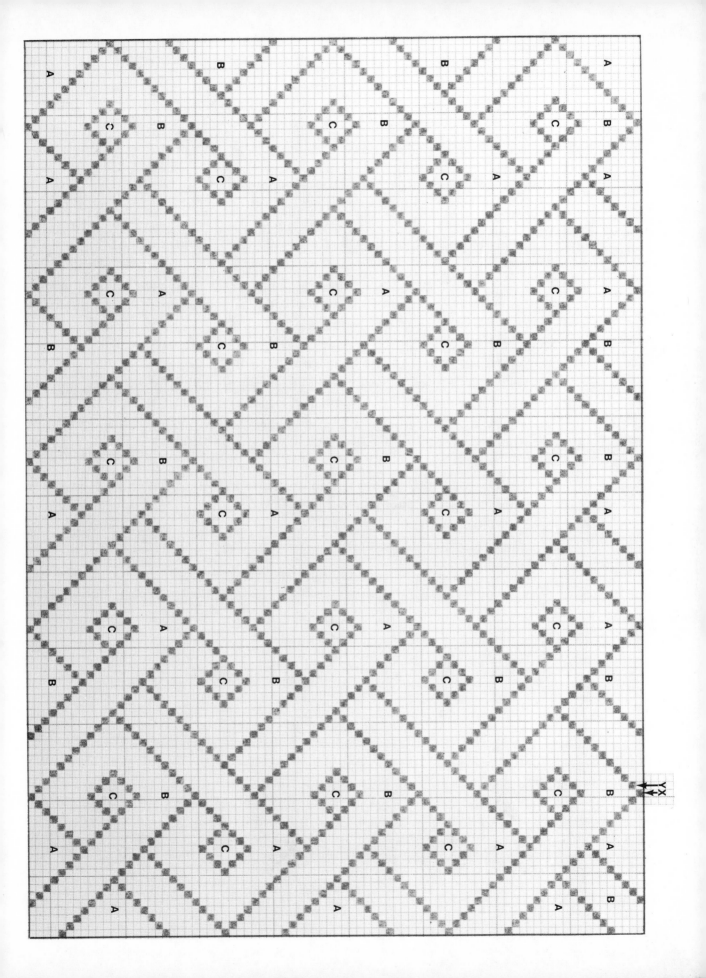

Trim the unworked canvas to ¾ inch from the needlepoint, and cut the canvas at an angle at the corners. Be careful not to cut into the needlepoint stitches.

Place the needlepoint face down, and place the two pieces of cardboard so that the outer edges of the needlepoint and the cardboard are together. With all-purpose glue, attach the unworked canvas margins to the cardboard, stretching the needlepoint tight, but not so tight that it buckles the cardboard. Use masking tape and straight pins to help hold the canvas margins in place until the glue becomes completely dry. Glue the margin to the back of the needlepoint along the top and bottom of the spine.

Cut two pieces of 1½-inch-wide grosgrain ribbon 2 inches longer than the height of the book cover. On the inside of the cover, glue down 1 inch of 1 piece of ribbon to the top center of the front and 1 inch of the other piece to the top center of the back.

Cut a piece of felt so that it covers the unfinished interior of the book cover. Glue it across the top, covering the glued-down ends of ribbon. Bring the ribbon down over the lining to form a loop, and glue 1 inch of the loose end to the bottom of the front and 1 inch of the other loose end to the bottom of the back.

Finish gluing the felt lining, over the glued-down ends of the ribbon, around the remaining edges.

LUGGAGE RACK STRAPS
Color photograph following page 104.

Needlepoint straps can transform an inexpensive wood luggage rack into an attractive, as well as practical accessory for a guest room.

Most luggage racks have 3 straps. Measure the width and length of one strap. Add an extra ¼ inch all around for the area to be worked. Mark the outline on canvas, leaving a margin of at least half the strap width on each side.

The design can be a motif from the curtains or wallpaper in the room, or it can be the wicker pattern, as shown on page 94, worked in harmonizing colors. This same pattern can be continued to make a belt or adapted as an allover design for a footstool, chair pad, cushion, or tote bag.

Materials Needed

Size of each finished luggage rack strap is approximately 3 inches x 18 inches.

Quantities of wool specified below are for 3-ply Persian wool needed for one strap. (Equivalent in tapestry yarn: 1 ounce Persian wool equals 40 yards.)

> #14 canvas, 8 inches x 23 inches
> #19 needle
> 2 ounces dark brown wool
> 2 ounces tan wool
> 1 ounce off-white wool
> ¾ yard fabric for backing (sailcloth or heavy linen)

Instructions

Bind the edges of the canvas with masking or adhesive tape. Mark the outline of the area to be worked in the center of the canvas.

This pattern is worked with the bargello stitch using the full 3 plys of Persian wool or full tapestry yarn.

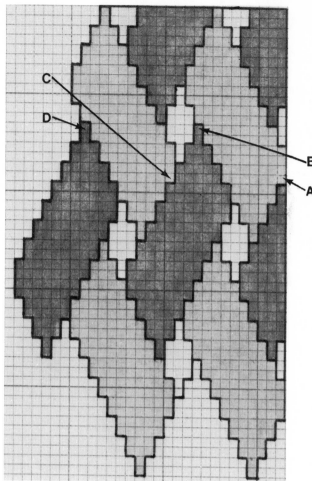

Starting a new wedge

Wedges in first color are started with top of canvas at the top; wedges in second color, with top of the canvas at the bottom. The arrows on the chart indicate the starting point of the first stitch in each of the first four wedges.

Mark the top of the canvas. Following the chart, start at the right edge of the outline, about 1½ inches from the top. Bring the needle from back to front of canvas (A on chart), leaving about an inch of yarn to be locked in by the first few stitches.

1st row: The stitch is vertical, and is made by skipping 3 holes and entering the 4th. Bring the needle back through the canvas in the next row to the left, 2nd hole down. Repeat these side stepping stitches 7 more times. On the 8th stitch bring the needle through to the front as before, in the next row to the left, 2nd hole down.

2nd row: Invert the canvas and insert the needle in the 4th hole directly above and bring it out in the next row to the left, 2nd hole down. This is a mesh that has already been worked by the 1st line. Continue side stepping up for 7 more stitches. On the 8th stitch, bring the needle to the front in the next row to the right, 2nd hole down.

The next stitch is made through the 4th hole directly above, bringing the needle out in the next row to the right, 2nd hole down.

3rd row: Invert the canvas and side step up to the left for 7 stitches. On the 8th stitch, bring the needle out in the next row to the left, 2nd hole down.

4th row: Invert the canvas, and side step up to the left for 8 stitches. On the 8th stitch, leave the needle at the back of the canvas. Turn the piece over, run the yarn under 5 or 6 worked stitches, and cut it off. You now have 4 rows of 8 stitches each.

Thread a needle with the 2nd color. Hold the strap so that the top of the canvas is at the bottom. Run the yarn under the worked stitches on the back so that you can bring the needle out through the same mesh as what is now the top of the 2nd stitch up in the last row worked (B on chart).

Wedge in second color:

1st row: Side step up (to the left) for 4 stitches to the left. On the 4th stitch bring the needle out in the next row to the right, 2nd hole down.

Make the next stitch through the 4th hole directly above, and bring it out in the next row to the right, 2nd hole down.

2nd row: Invert the canvas, and side step up to the left for 3 additional stitches. Bring the needle out in the next row to the left, 2nd hole down.

3rd row: Invert the canvas, and side step up 4 stitches.

Repeat as with rows 1 and 2 until you have 8 diagonal lines of 4 stitches each. With the last stitch, run the yarn under some stitches on the back, and cut it off.

Return to the 1st color. Holding the strap with the top up, run the yarn under the back stitches so that it can be brought out through the same mesh as the top of the 4th stitch down at the left of the 2nd color wedge (C on chart).

Side step up to the left for 8 stitches. You can see you are forming a wedge shape exactly like the first one. Complete it in the same way, and then repeat the 2nd color as before starting at D. Start the next wedge at E.

You now have the pattern set up for the entire luggage strap. When you have filled in the entire outlined area with this criss-cross pattern, go back and fill in the small, off-white diamond shapes, using the same stitch. Make two more straps exactly like this one.

Finishing

Fold the unworked edges under, and stitch them together with a strong thread. Press on the wrong side with a hot iron and a damp cloth. (A narrow piece, worked in bargello, rarely needs blocking.) Cover the back with a strip of fabric. (Stitching is better than gluing here.) Remove the straps that came on the luggage rack and tack on the needlepoint straps.

PATCHWORK CHRISTMAS STOCKING
Color photograph following page 104.

A needlepoint Christmas stocking is a charming way to present a small gift that may be an heirloom decoration for years to come. The patchwork pattern of Christmas motifs is a good way to use leftover yarn.

The stocking shown in the color photograph is worked with 2 plys of Persian yarn on #12 canvas; however, the amounts of yarn given below are adequate to work with the full 3-ply Persian yarn on #10 canvas. If you use #10 canvas, the stocking will be slightly larger when finished.

Materials Needed

Size of finished Christmas stocking is approximately 6 inches wide x 9 inches long.

Quantities of wool specified below are for 3-ply Persian wool. (Equivalent in tapestry yarn: 1 ounce Persian wool equals 40 yards; 1 strand equals 30 inches.)

> #12 canvas, 13 inches x 15 inches
> #18 needle
> ½ ounce black wool (Color A)
> ½ ounce blue wool (Color B)
> 5 strands lavender wool (Color C)
> ½ ounce red wool (Color D)
> 10 strands dark orange wool (Color E)
> 10 strands light orange wool (Color F)
> 15 strands pink wool (Color G)
> 15 strands dark green wool (Color H)
> ½ ounce light green wool (Color I)
> ½ ounce white wool (Color J)
> ¼ yard fabric for lining—light silk or faille that matches or
>   harmonizes with one of the yarn colors

All-purpose glue

Felt for backing (in harmonizing color)

Instructions

Bind the edges of the canvas with masking or adhesive tape. Mark the outline of the working area in the center of the canvas. Use 2 plys of the Persian wool or full tapestry yarn.

Begin in the upper right-hand corner of the design. Following the chart, work the pattern in either the basket-weave or continental method, or in a combination of the two because single lines cannot be done in basket weave.

Finishing

After the completed work has been blocked (see page 55), trim the canvas around the edge of the needlepoint, leaving a ½-inch margin of unworked canvas. Turn the canvas margins to the back, and stitch them by hand to the back of the needlepoint. Cut two pieces of the lining material about the same size as the needlepoint. Stitch the lining pieces together, ½ inch from the edge all around, but leave the top open.

Cut a piece of felt the shape and size of the finished stocking. Stitch the edges of the felt and the needlepoint pieces together, leaving the top open. Insert the lining. Turn the top edges of the lining in, and stitch the lining opening to the front and to the back.

A loop of yarn or felt attached to the top of the stocking can be used for hanging. Or buy an inexpensive gold chain bracelet and attach the fastener to the top for a fancier (and more permanent) loop.

8 ∽

Wall Hangings

The art of tapestry parallels that of needlepoint, and although the mechanics are different, both crafts have been used interchangeably throughout the ages. Tapestry and needlepoint chairs share museum space, as do historical wall hangings of both arts. Both have enjoyed a revival in the 20th century, and modern tapestries are becoming more and more popular as wall decorations. It is not suggested that a beginner attempt to reproduce the intricate designs of museum tapestries; however, large and decorative works are not beyond the scope of even the most modest artist.

Popular objects in this category include framed needlepoint pictures, family crests, family trees, mottoes, and bellpulls. Bellpulls no longer summon a servant, but they can serve the purpose of decorating a narrow space or covering a mechanical object, such as the house phone in an apartment foyer.

You can reproduce almost anything in a needlepoint picture—a portrait of a favorite dog or country house, an abstraction, or floral designs from a Victorian bouquet of roses to the simplified single rose described on the next page. Children's books are filled with marvelous ideas for needlepoint pictures to decorate a child's room. And many religious pictures are worked in needlepoint and used as hangings.

Mottoes can be serious or amusing and make wonderful wall hangings. These are usually framed.

GIANT ROSE
Color photograph following page 104.

This is a perfect project for a beginner. It can be framed as a picture or serve as a pillow design. The rose has been worked in shades of pink, but it would be equally attractive in other colors. The tone values of dark, medium, light, and white, however, should be kept more or less as they are here.

Materials Needed

Size of finished Giant Rose is approximately 13 inches x 13 inches.

Quantities of wool specified below are for rug wool. (Equivalent in other heavy wools or acrylic rug yarn: 1 ounce rug wool equals about 15⅓ yards; 1 strand equals 30 inches.)

> #5 canvas, 19 inches x 19 inches
> #13 rug needle
> 10 ounces white wool (Color A)
> 2 ounces pink wool (Color B)
> 7 strands dark pink wool (Color C)
> 1½ ounces red wool (Color D)
> 1 ounce dark green wool (Color E)
> 8 strands purple wool (Color F)
> 10 strands light green wool (Color G)
> 2 strands orange wool (Color H)
> Picture frame
> ¼-inch plywood to fit frame
> Finishing nails
> Heavy paper for backing
> All-purpose glue
> Glass (optional)

Instructions

The Giant Rose is worked on #5 mesh canvas with rug wool using the half-cross stitch. Five mesh canvas has a double-thread weave,

but you ignore the smaller openings. The canvas should be held so that the 2 threads closest together are in a vertical position. If the piece of canvas has a selvage, it should be at the side, never the top or bottom.

If you plan to frame the picture, find a frame close to the size of the finished piece. If you prefer a larger size, a mat can be used to fill a larger frame, or the background of the needlepoint can be extended.

Bind the edges with masking or adhesive tape. Mark the outline of the area to be worked in the center of the canvas.

For this project, it is easier to work the flower first and then the background. Unlike regular needlepoint wool, rug wool or jumbo yarn does not show filaments of other colors when pulled through to the front, so doing the flower first will not cause any discoloration of the white background.

Each square on the chart represents 1 stitch. Mark one in the upper left-hand corner of the rose as a place to begin. Count down and over on the chart, then the same number of threads on the canvas to locate your 1st stitch.

Bring the wool through from the back leaving about an inch of yarn to be locked in with the first few stitches. Insert the needle diagonally into the adjacent upper-right large square (ignore the smaller squares formed by the double threads) and bring it out in the large hole directly below. Continue this half-cross stitch working from left to right for the number of squares (stitches) shown on the chart. Invert the canvas for the next row. Follow this procedure until the color area you started is filled in to match the chart.

To start the next color area, bury the end of the yarn under 5 or 6 of the already worked stitches on the back. Bring the needle out where you wish the 1st stitch to begin.

Fill in all the colors, counting the stitches on the chart to guide you. Then fill in the background, still using the half-cross method.

Finishing

When the needlepoint is finished and blocked (see page 55), cut a piece of 1/4-inch plywood 1/2 inch smaller in width and height than the opening of the picture frame. (The smaller dimensions of the wood panel allow for the thickness of the needlepoint.)

Place the needlepoint face down, and center the plywood on top of it. Bring the unworked edges of the canvas to the back, and tack or staple them to the plywood. Place the mounted needlework in the frame, and toe nail it (drive nails in horizontally) to hold the piece in place. A piece of wrapping paper should be glued to the back of the frame to cover the back of the needlepoint and plywood.

Some people prefer to have needlepoint pieces framed with glass to protect them, but others feel that the rich texture of the piece is too beautiful to mask in this way. The choice is yours.

If you want to use this design for a pillow, see instructions for finishing on page 121. For a box pillow, see page 124.

Motto Pin Cushion (p. 66); Anemone Coaster (p. 58); Monogrammed Napkin Ring (p. 77).

Three Kitchen Plaques: Pea Pods (p. 105); Mushrooms (p. 105); Strawberries (p. 105).

Wicker Design
Luggage Rack Straps (p. 93)

Mushroom Door Stop (p. 86).

Giant Rose Picture (p. 101); Tahiti Pillow (p. 120).

Motto Pillow (p. 122); Christmas Stocking (p. 97); Pomegranate Bellpull (p. 111).

Initialed Bookmark (p. 74); Rug Square (p. 131); Geometric Book Cover (p. 89).

(Left to right) Bargello Clutch Bag (p. 80); **Signal-flag** Belt (p. 69); Flame-stitch Eyeglass Case (p. 61).

Geometric Tie-on Pad (p. 116).

THREE KITCHEN PLAQUES
Color photograph following page 104.

The three small plaques illustrated are fun to do as an experiment because each combines the tent stitch with a different background stitch. When framed, they make a charming addition to a kitchen or an informal dining area. The designs can be adapted for other uses, too—slipcovers for kitchen bookends or attractive hot pads.

Materials Needed

Size of each finished plaque is approximately 5 inches x 7 inches.

Quantities of wool specified below are for 3-ply Persian wool. (Equivalent in tapestry yarn: 1 ounce Persian wool equals 40 yards; 1 strand equals 30 inches.)

> #12 canvas, 9 inches x 11 inches (for each plaque)
> #18 needle
>
> ### PEAPODS
> 1 strand light green wool (Color A)
> 5 strands dark green wool (Color B)
> 4 strands chartreuse wool (Color C)
> 5 strands white wool (Color D)
> 1 ounce turquoise wool (Color E)
>
> ### MUSHROOMS
> 6 strands white wool (Color A)
> 4 strands gray wool (Color B)
> 1 strand light brown wool (Color C)
> 1 strand orange wool (Color D)
> 1 ounce bright green wool (Color E)
>
> ### STRAWBERRIES
> 8 strands pink wool (Color A)
> 2 strands yellow wool (Color B)

5 strands green wool (Color C)

1½ ounces white wool (Color D)

3 5-inch x 7-inch picture frames (one for each picture)

Instructions

Bind the edges of the canvas with masking or adhesive tape. Mark the outline of the area to be worked in the center of the canvas. Follow the design charts on pages 107, 108, and 109.

PEAPODS

Work the peapods, using either the continental or basket-weave method, and using 2 plys of the 3-ply wool.

The background is filled in with a variation of the slanting Gobelin stitch, using the full 3-ply wool. The variation is: in the 1st row skip 2 holes, and slant stitches from lower left to upper right; in the 2nd row skip 1 hole, and slant stitches in the opposite direction. This gives a ribbed herringbone effect. To make background conform with edges of design, some small areas will have to be filled in with small stitches slanting in the same direction as the larger stitches in the row so that the ribbed effect is maintained.

MUSHROOMS

The mushrooms are worked in either continental or basket-weave method, using 2 plys of the 3-ply wool.

The background is filled in with the Parisian stitch, using the full 3-ply wool. (If you prefer you may use Brick stitch, Hungarian stitch, or Mosaic stitch for the background.)

STRAWBERRIES

The strawberries are worked in either the continental or basket-weave method, using 2 plys of the 3-ply wool. The yellow "seeds" are then overstitched here and there using a popcorn knot, which is made in this way: lock the yellow yarn under a few worked stitches on the back and bring it out to the front where you want the "seed" to be. Make a loop of the yarn as near the face of the strawberry as possible, and put the needle through it, forming a very loose knot. Hold the yarn up with your left hand, and with your needle work the knot down until it forms a tight knot on the surface of the strawberry. Insert the needle in the adjoining upper-right square. Run the

Peapods

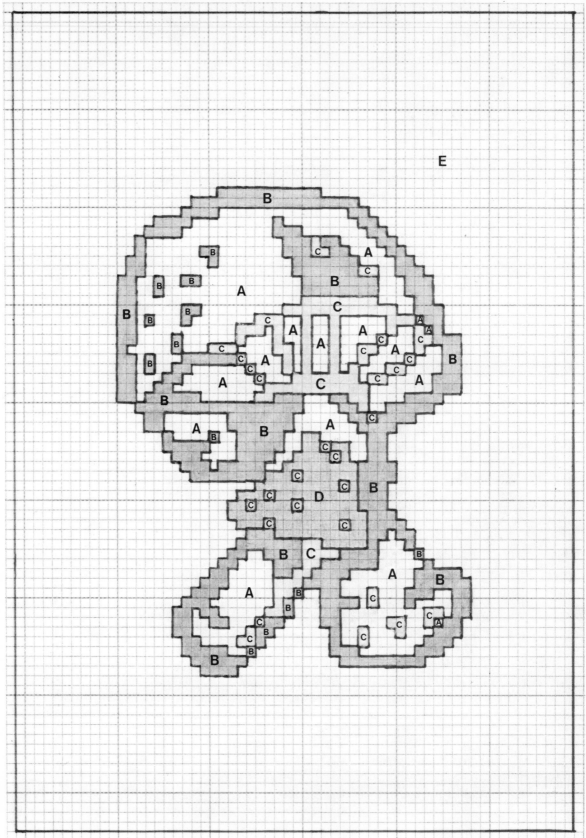

Mushrooms

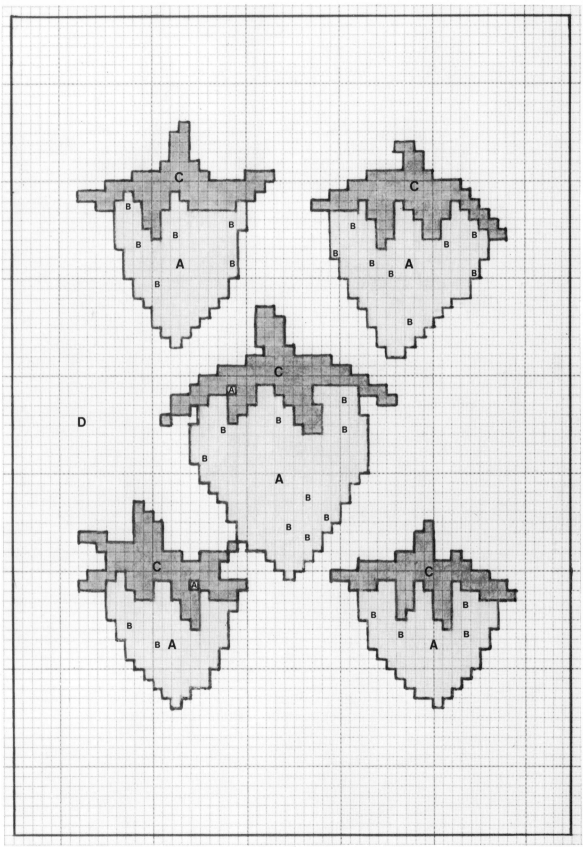

Strawberries

yarn under a few stitches to the next location, and make another "seed," and so forth.

The background is worked in a version of the Scotch stitch forming a checkerboard pattern. Or you can use the Mosaic stitch, the Hungarian stitch, or the Brick stitch for the background. Use the full 3-ply wool for any of these stitches.

Finishing

Pressing on the wrong side with a steam iron or a hot iron and a damp pressing cloth will probably be all the blocking that is necessary. The various background stitches suggested do not pull the canvas out of shape.

If your picture frame has a cardboard filler, it will be necessary to trim it slightly to allow for the thickness of the needlepoint. Trim the unworked edges of the canvas to ½ inch, clip the corners out, and glue the edges to the cardboard. Fit into the frame, and glue a piece of wrapping paper to the back.

POMEGRANATE BELLPULL
Color photograph following page 104.

The pomegranate bellpull is designed with a vertical repeat pattern. The chart shows the design repeat, which continues down the length of the piece.

Materials Needed

Size of finished bellpull is approximately 5 inches x 46 inches.

Quantities of wool specified below are for 3-ply Persian wool. (Equivalent in tapestry yarn: 1 ounce Persian wool equals 40 yards.)

> #10 canvas, 11 inches x 54 inches
> #17 needle
> 3 ounces green wool (Color A)
> 2 ounces pink wool (Color B)
> 1½ ounces orange wool (Color C)
> 4 ounces brown wool (Color D)
> ¼ yard (54 inches wide) or 1½ yards (36 inches wide) fabric
>   for backing (heavy linen, sailcloth, or felt)
> Wood (thin doweling or a tongue depressor) for top bar
> Brass curtain ring (1½ inches in diameter)
> For the tassels: 2 ounces each of the pink and orange wools

Instructions

Bind the edges of the canvas with masking or adhesive tape. Mark the outline of the area to be worked in the center of the canvas.

Work with full 3 plys of Persian wool or full tapestry yarn.

Roll the canvas up to about 10 inches from the top, and pin it on each side. This makes it much easier to handle.

Start the design 2 inches from the top of the outline and 10 threads over from the right side. This design is easiest to work with the basket-weave method so that you will not have to invert the canvas at the end of each row.

Follow the pattern by counting the stitches on the chart and un-

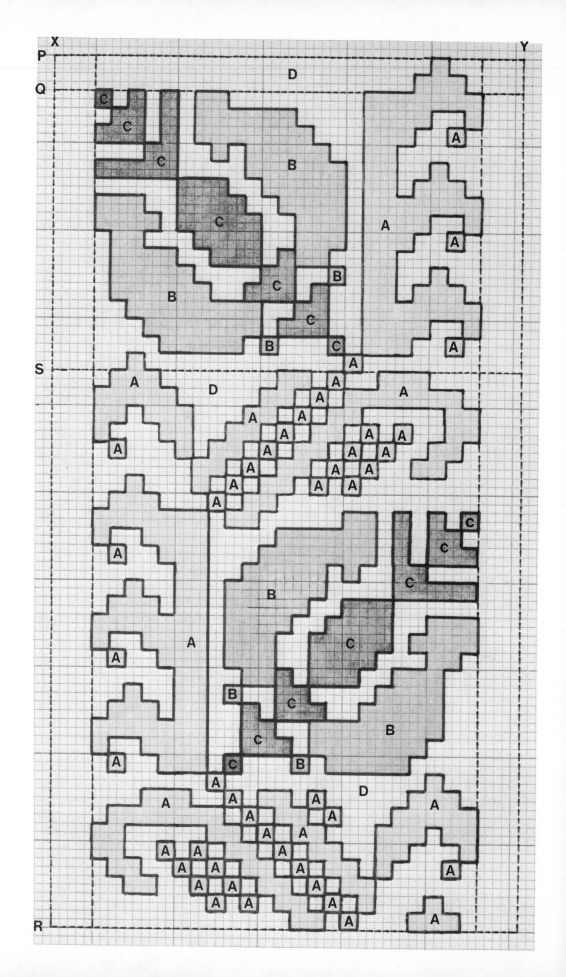

rolling the canvas as you progress. Work from P to Q once, repeat Q to R 4 times, then do Q to S once.

When you have completed the repeats of the design in accordance with instructions above, go back to the top and fill in the background with the basket-weave method. The background should start 2 inches above and end 1 inch below the design and should extend 5 stitches to the right and left (X and Y on chart).

Finishing

When blocking the finished piece (see page 55), you may have to use the inside of a closet door if there is not a large enough piece of plywood available. If the piece is only a little out of shape, pressing it on the wrong side with a steam iron or a hot iron and a damp pressing cloth will probably be sufficient.

Trim the unworked canvas margins to about 1 inch beyond the worked area. Turn the canvas margins to the back, and stitch them by hand to the back of the needlepoint. If the corners seem to be too thick, they can be notched out.

Cut a piece of fabric for backing with a ½-inch seam allowance. Turn seam allowance under, and press or baste to the back of the fabric. Stitch the backing to the needlepoint with small invisible stitches.

To finish the bellpull, turn back a hem at the top deep enough to cover a thin piece of wood such as a tongue depressor. Insert the wood, and sew up the sides of the hem. Attach a brass curtain ring at the top center by sewing through the two thicknesses of needlepoint.

To make the decorative tassels for the bottom, cut a piece of heavy cardboard 5 inches square. Mix 1 ounce each of the pink and orange yarns and wrap them completely around the piece of cardboard. Take three strands of one of the above colors, and tie them through the loop of yarn at the top of the cardboard. Next, cut off the tag ends at the edge of the cardboard, and then cut the loops of yarn at the bottom as well. Slide wool off cardboard and tightly wrap another strand of yarn around the tassel 1½ inches down from the top. Tie it and tuck in the ends. Make the second tassel in the same manner. Braid the three strands at the top of each tassel, and attach a tassel to each corner of the bottom of the bellpull.

9 ⌒

Chair Seats

The two easiest chair coverings to be made, without the help of a professional upholsterer, are the tie-on pad and the slip seat.

A chair with a wooden or rush seat is certainly made more comfortable and attractive with a needlepoint pad. The pattern of the pad can easily be marked and cut from brown wrapping paper to conform to the shape of the chair. A design can then be adapted to fit the scale, the design of the chair, and its surroundings. Unless the chair seat needs to be made higher, the pad should be made thin with a knife edge or a 1-inch boxing. The pad can be secured to the chair by cords with tassels or with flat ties made from the material used on the underside of the pad.

Slip seats are easily removed from chairs or benches by removing the screws from the underside. If the seats have been upholstered, the piece of material you are replacing can serve as a pattern for the new needlepoint covering. If not, carefully measure the exposed surface to be covered with a tape measure, including the thickness of the seat from edge to edge. Then allow at least 2 inches of canvas on all four sides.

Outline the exposed area to be worked in needlepoint. The design can then be suitably selected and applied to the size and shape of the cover. In working the design, the stitching should extend an inch beyond the outline.

When the work has been finished and blocked (see page 55), center the canvas on the chair seat and pin it at the four corners to avoid slipping. Turn the seat over and tack the canvas about ½ inch from the edge across the back in four places. (A strong staple gun can be used to attach the canvas.) Now pull the canvas tightly to the front and tack it to the underside of the seat. Pull it firmly from side to side and tack the sides. Turn the corners neatly by tacking the left front corner first and then the right back corner. The opposite corners are done next. Check the top side of the seat to be certain it is true, then tack about every ½ inch all around. Any excess canvas should be trimmed off about ½ inch from the tacks.

Cut a piece of dark muslin to cover the bottom of the seat. Fold in the edges and tack it about ¼ inch from the edge to avoid the other tacks.

Upholstered chairs or benches finished with nailheads, welting, or gimp should be planned professionally from the start. The upholsterer who will finish the chair will supply a paper pattern for the cover, taking into consideration all the technicalities involved. The design can then be plotted out on this pattern so that when it is completed, you may be sure it will fit.

The pattern selected for the tie-on pad project that follows is a geometric design that is suitable for either country or city living. It is also an excellent design for a rug.

GEOMETRIC TIE-ON PAD
Color photograph following page 104.

Materials Needed

The size of the canvas and quantity of wool depends on the size of the pad. The quantities listed here are for a 12-inch x 16-inch pad. Adjust amounts to fit size of pad needed for your chair.

Quantities of wool specified below are for rug wool. (Equivalent in other heavy wools or acrylic rug yarn: 1 ounce rug wool equals about 15⅓ yards.)

> #3 canvas, 16 inches x 20 inches
> #13 rug needle
> 10 ounces blue wool (Color A)
> 10 ounces brown wool (Color B)
> 10 ounces white wool (Color C)
> ½ yard sturdy fabric, such as upholstery-weight linen or heavy felt, for backing and ties
> Stuffing material (shredded foam, Dacron® polyester fiberfill, or cotton batting)
> 1¾ yards upholstery welting in any one of the 3 colors

Instructions

Bind the edges of the canvas with masking or adhesive tape. Mark the outline of the area to be worked in the center of the canvas.

The design is cross-stitched with rug wool. Fold the canvas in four to find its center. Mark it with a dot. Start the design at the center and continue the pattern as established on the chart to fit the size and shape of your chair pad.

Finishing

After the finished piece has been blocked (see page 55), trim the unworked canvas to ½ inch. Cut a piece from the backing material

to conform to the shape of the finished needlepoint, allowing ½-inch seam allowance all around.

Cut two strips of the backing material 20 inches x 2¼ inches for ties. (If you use felt for the ties, cut strips 20 inches x ¾ inch. No allowance for finishing is needed.) To make the fabric ties, fold the strip lengthwise into thirds. Turn under ¼ inch at raw edge. Press and stitch by hand along this turned-in edge with small, invisible stitches. Turn in ¼ inch at each end and stitch closed.

For a welt edge, place needlepoint and backing right sides together with welting sandwiched between, raw edges facing out. Baste as close to cord as possible. Sew together by hand or machine on three sides. Trim excess canvas ¼ inch from stitching line. Reverse the casing, and fill with suitable stuffing. Sew the opening together by hand close to the edges of the two pieces. Catch threads just inside the edges so that stitches are invisible. (If you want to finish the seat pad with a box edge, see instructions on page 124.)

Stitching across the center of the tie, attach one tie to each of the two back corners of the needlepoint pad.

This design can also be used effectively for a rug. To make a small, one-piece rug, just draw an outline of the size you want on the canvas. Allow a 2½-inch margin all around. Bind the edges of the canvas with masking or adhesive tape. Start the design in the center as you would for the tie-on chair pad. Following the chart, continue the design to within 4 rows of the outline. Then fill in the 4 rows with a border of 1 color, using the same stitch as you used for the rug.

To make rug squares, draw the outline of a 12-inch or 14-inch square on the canvas. Allow a 2½-inch margin all around. Bind the edges of the canvas with masking or adhesive tape. Start from the center of the square and work the design, following the chart to within 2 rows of the outline. Then fill in the 2 rows with a border of 1 of the darker colors, using the same stitch as you used for the rug.

After you have finished the number of squares you need, block them (see page 55) and follow the directions for finishing a rug on page 133.

The outside border for this rug should be a simple one—4 rows of the darkest color worked in the same stitch as you used for the rug. Follow instructions on pages 133-134 for making a border.

10

Pillows

As a color accent in any room, nothing does the job quite like a pillow. In addition, it serves many useful functions—makes a deep sofa or chair more comfortably shallow, props up an elbow, supports a tired back, softens the look of a room. In other words, when you make a needlepoint pillow you have something of value and an art object besides.

Many of the designs used in the other projects in the book can be adapted to make pillows. You may want to use a larger mesh canvas with a heavier yarn—or you may decide to use part of a design as a center motif and just extend the background. The allover designs, such as the ones used in the luggage rack strap or the geometric book cover or the repeat pattern of the chair seat, would be effective and easy to convert. The bargello designs used in the clutch bag or the flame stitch used in the eyeglass case would make attractive patterns for pillows, too. And, of course, you can enjoy the added pleasure of creating your own color combinations to suit your own taste and decor.

The usual sizes for square sofa pillows are 12 inches x 12 inches, 14 inches x 14 inches, 16 inches x 16 inches, 18 inches x 18 inches. Pillows for use on the floor should be 24 inches x 24 inches. Of course, pillows can also be oblong or round. Small oblong pillows are especially attractive and comfortable to use on upholstered chairs.

TAHITI PILLOW
Color photograph following page 104.

Try sketching your own design for this pillow. Use the color photograph as a guide—or create your own overall pattern of free-form flowers. First draw an outline of the size of the pillow you want on drawing paper. (The one in the photograph is 16 inches x 16 inches.) The directions on page 15 will tell you how to paint a design and transfer it to canvas. This may start you on a creative approach to needlepoint that will provide an endless source of satisfaction and pleasure. You do not have to be a trained artist to do this. Let yourself go; you may have more talent than you think. (If you prefer to use the design shown, enlarge the drawing on the opposite page. Draw 2-inch squares within the outline of the pillow and copy the pattern as it appears within each small square.)

Materials Needed

(For the design shown in the color photograph.)

Quantities of wool specified below are for 3-ply Persian wool. (Equivalent in tapestry yarn: 1 ounce Persian wool equals 40 yards; 1 strand equals 30 inches.)

> #10 canvas, 21 inches x 21 inches
> #17 needle
> 1 ounce blue wool
> 2 ounces green wool
> 2 ounces red wool
> 2 ounces pink wool
> 2 ounces yellow wool
> 3 ounces violet wool
> 7 strands black wool
> Fabric for backing—velveteen, felt, sailcloth, or suede cloth
>   (size of pillow plus ½-inch seam allowance all around)
> Stuffing material (feathers, Dacron® polyester fiberfill, or
>   shredded foam)

Instructions

Bind the edges of the canvas with masking or adhesive tape. Mark the outline of the area to be worked in the center of the canvas.

The free forms of the flowers and foliage need not follow any precise mesh count. The stitches can be done in either the basket-weave or continental method. Use the full 3-ply Persian or full tapestry yarn.

Finishing

After the work is complete, block the piece according to the blocking instructions on page 55.

Cut a piece of backing fabric the same size as the finished needlepoint, plus a ½-inch seam allowance all around. Place the canvas face to face with the backing, right sides together. Pin or baste together. Sew together by hand or machine on three sides. Trim excess canvas ¼ inch from stitching line.

Reverse the pillow, and fill with stuffing material.

Sew the edges of the open end together by hand. (Catch threads just inside the turned-in edges so that stitches are invisible.)

Each square = 2-inch square

MOTTO PILLOW
Color photograph following page 104.

Almost anything worth saying can be said colorfully and amusingly in needlepoint. A familiar motto can be worked into a pillow top or an appropriate message can be stitched into a small hanging for a door or wall. A needlepoint sampler is a timeless gift. Make one for a new mother with the baby's name, birth date, and place of birth; or as a wedding gift, designed with the name of the bride and groom and the date of the marriage. If you are ambitious, you might enjoy designing a family tree for yourself or for someone you love. (Or make a motto pincushion; see page 66.)

The instructions below are for a pillow. If you prefer to frame the piece, see instructions on page 104. If you want to make a small hanging message (see suggestions on page 126), just mount the needlepoint on cardboard and attach a piece of velvet ribbon as a "hanger." (For these small pieces, it is better to work on #12 or #14 canvas.)

The motto on the pillow photographed is: "Don't worry; it always happens." (Other mottoes are suggested on page 124.) Since the letters vary in color, you may find this a fine project for using up odd bits of wool. To make the pillow exactly as it appears in the photograph use the colors listed below. Or you may select any colors you like.

If you choose another motto, work it out on graph paper first, using one of the alphabets on pages 126, 127, or 128 as a guide. Instructions for making graph-paper charts can be found on page 13.

Materials Needed

Size of finished pillow is approximately 9½ inches wide x 14 inches long by 1¼ inches high.

Quantities of wool specified below are for 3-ply Persian wool. (Equivalent in tapestry yarn: 1 ounce Persian wool equals 40 yards; 1 strand equals 30 inches.)

#10 canvas, 14 inches x 19 inches

#17 needle

5 ounces white wool (background, Color A)

½ ounce yellow wool (Color B)

6 strands gold wool (Color C)

½ ounce orange wool (Color D)

1 ounce pink wool (Color E)

8 strands red wool (Color F)

½ ounce lavender wool (Color G)

6 strands purple wool (Color H)

8 strands light blue wool (Color I)

8 strands dark blue wool (Color J)

6 strands light green wool (Color K)

3 strands dark green wool (Color L)

To finish as pillow: ½ yard 36-inch fabric for backing (velveteen, felt, sailcloth, suede cloth, or faille silk are suggested)

Stuffing material (feathers, Dacron® polyester fiberfill, or shredded foam)

Instructions

Bind the edges of the canvas with masking or adhesive tape. Mark the outline of the area to be worked in the center of the canvas.

Transfer the border and the lettering from the chart on page 125 to the canvas with a waterproof marker or with a small brush and acrylic paint thinned with water.

Each marked square in the chart represents a stitch. The top right stitch of the left section of the *D* is worked over the intersection of the 13th thread down from the top of the background area and the 9th thread from the left of the background area edge. When you have established this position you will have no difficulty in placing the rest of the lettering. Just count the filled-in squares on the chart and mark a stitch (an intersection of threads) on the canvas for each square.

Fill in the background using the basket-weave or the continental method. Then do the motto. Letters are usually worked in a combination of basket-weave and continental methods. The important thing is to have a stitch for each square marked on the chart.

When the motto is finished, carefully trim off any fuzzy tag ends on the back so that they will not show up later on the surface of the completed piece.

The border is made with a series of rows done in the Gobelin stitch. The outer row skips 3 holes, and the other 4 rows skip only 1 hole (see photograph).

This pillow was made with a 1¼-inch box edge, which requires a strip of fabric 2½ inches wide x 49 inches long. The backing requires a piece 10½ inches x 15 inches. These sizes include a ½-inch seam allowance all around.

Finishing

When the needlepoint has been blocked (see page 55), trim the unworked canvas margin to ½ inch. Sew the needlepoint to the boxing (right sides together) either by hand or machine along the last row of needlepoint. Then sew the other edge of the boxing to the backing in the same way, leaving an end open to insert the stuffing. Turn the pillow right side out, and fill with stuffing material. Sew the open end together by hand with small invisible stitches.

Here are some favorite old mottoes you may want to use:

> *WHEN THIS YOU SEE THINK OF ME*
> *LOVE WILL FIND A WAY*
> *FORGIVEN AND FORGOTTEN*
> *LOVE ME, LOVE MY DOG*
> *NEVER SAY DIE*
> *WOMAN'S WORK IS NEVER DONE*
> *A PENNY FOR YOUR THOUGHTS*
> *PRACTICE MAKES PERFECT*
> *MY HOUSE IS MY CASTLE*
> *IS LIFE UPHILL ALL THE WAY (work on a slant)*
> *BETTER LATE THAN NEVER*
> *LOVE MAKES THE WORLD GO ROUND*
> *A FRIEND IN NEED IS A FRIEND INDEED*

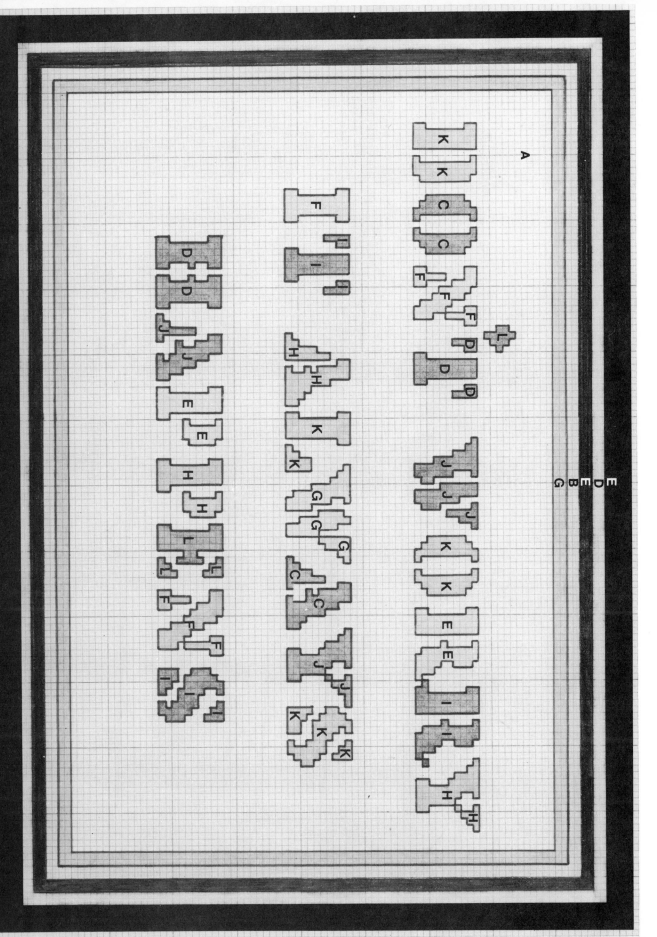

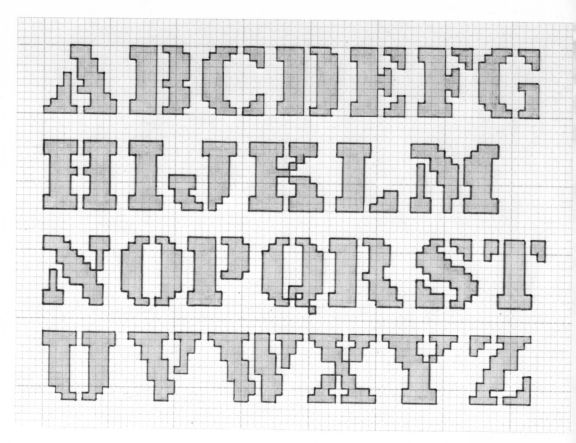

For a little hanging message, you may want to try something original that is particularly appropriate. Below are some ideas to start you thinking:

PLEASE COME IN
SH-SH; BABY'S SLEEPING
GO AWAY. I'M HAVING A BAD DAY
THE WINNER!
WORLD'S BEST (GOLFER, HUSBAND, FISHERMAN, ETC.)
THE   (FAMILY NAME)   SAY "MERRY CHRISTMAS"
I'M PROUD OF YOU
MAN AT WORK
REMEMBER TO WRITE
CAUTION: ROOM UNDER REPAIR

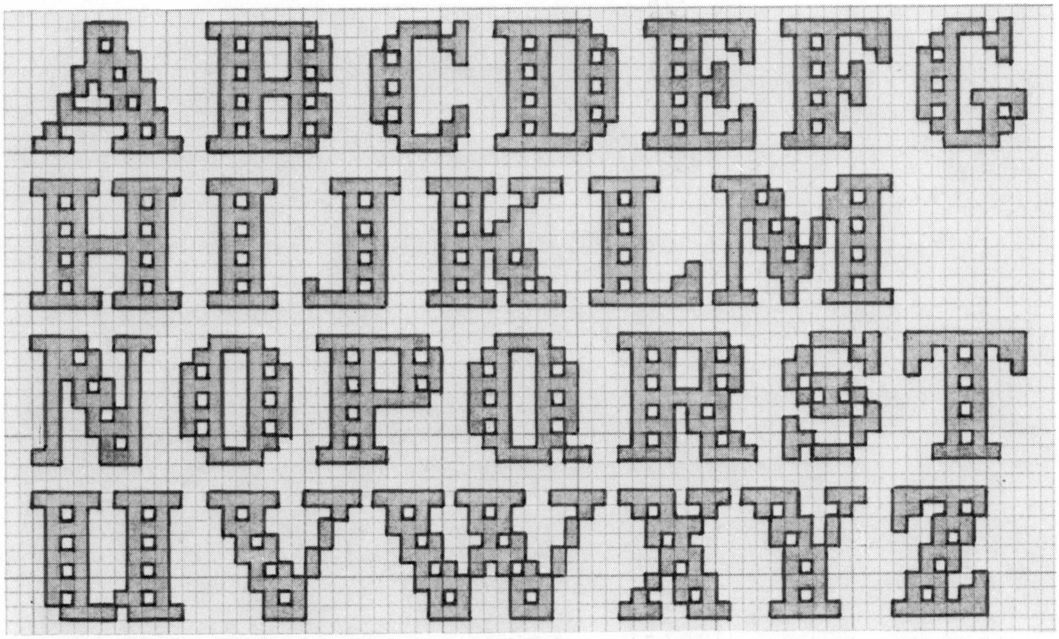

ABCDEFG
HIJKLM
NOPQRST
UVWXYZ

ABCDEFG
HIJKLM
NOPQRST
UVWXYZ-
1234567890

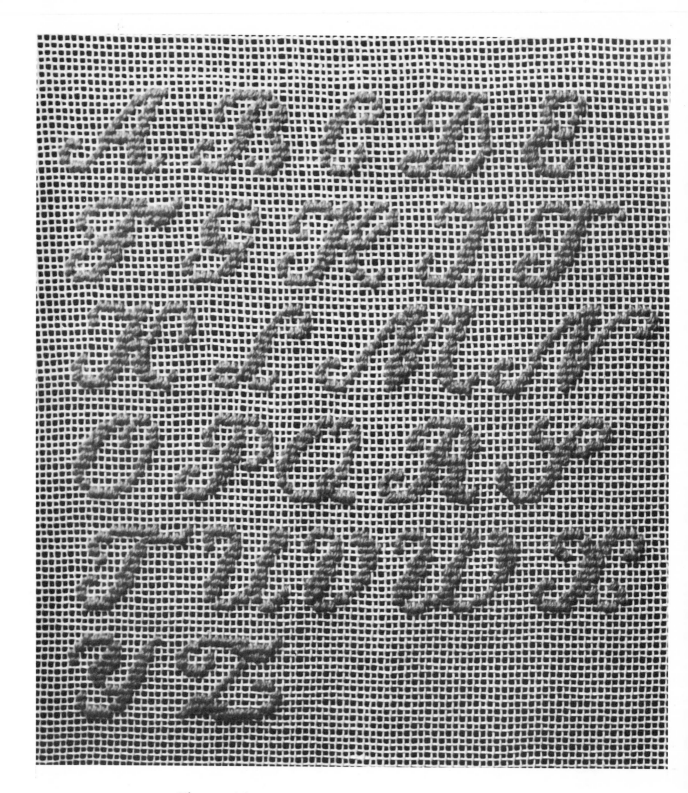

The graceful curves of a script alphabet reproduced on canvas

11

Rugs

A needlepoint rug made with modern mothproof wool on good strong canvas may still be around a hundred years from now, a treasured heirloom that keeps increasing in value all the time.

Large rugs can be made either in squares or strips that are sewn or overstitched together to create the finished size. Rug squares are more portable than strips and therefore more convenient to work.

If you use #5 mesh stitched with rug wool, or #3 mesh cross-stitched with rug wool, you can make a rug far more quickly than you could if you made it in ordinary needlepoint; but of course its texture will be more casual.

When buying wool for a rug, it is important to buy all the background wool required for the project at one time. Dye lots seldom match exactly, and you may find it difficult to buy just the color you want later on.

Small hearth or bedside rugs represent more challenge than a pillow, yet completing them need not be a more time-consuming project. They can be worked in one piece, eliminating the sewing or stitching time in finishing. The design should be in keeping with the surroundings, but because the rug is small and usually occupies a conspicuous location in the room, it can be a highly decorative accent.

Large rugs represent an investment of a great deal of time and money, so they should be carefully thought out and planned. It is not a good idea to make a rug to fit an odd-sized room or area because it might prove to be unusable in another location. Average sizes are 2 feet x 3 feet, 3 feet x 5 feet, 4 feet x 6 feet, 5 feet x 7 feet, 8 feet x 10 feet, 9 feet x 12 feet. These sizes are more or less standard and are suitable for many areas.

Rugs should be designed with borders, whether the border is worked on the same piece of canvas as the center field or worked separately. The border may be in plain bands of color or a simplified design to frame the central motif. On the other hand, a rug can have a simple center with an elaborate border, depending upon other decorative elements in the room.

Another needlepoint rug project you may want to consider is stair treads—which can transform a stairway into a work of art. The conservative method is to make a needlepoint pad for each stair tread. The pad should be the same depth as the tread and 3 inches narrower on either side. (If the stair curves, some of the treads must be shaped to fit the wedge-shaped steps, of course.) A more lavish way to decorate stairs is to make a runner to fit the entire stairway. One method used is to make the treads a different design from the risers. Looking up the stairs one sees the design on the risers, and looking down the stairs one sees something quite different!

RUG SQUARE USING INTERLOCKING RIBBON DESIGN

Color photograph following page 104.

This design is suitable to use with almost any style of decoration. Also, the rug square is small enough to be easily transported and worked.

The 9-inch square described below would also make an attractive top for a tiny cushion. Or you can use this design to make any size pillow if you use a larger piece of canvas, center the design, and add to the outside border.

Materials Needed

Size of finished rug square is approximately 9 inches x 9 inches.

Quantities of wool specified are for rug wool needed for each square. (Equivalent in other heavy wools or acrylic rug yarn: 1 ounce rug wool equals about 15⅓ yards.)

> #5 canvas, 12 inches x 12 inches
> #13 rug needle
> 2 ounces green wool (Color A)
> 2 ounces orange wool (Color B)
> 4 ounces white wool (Color C)

Note: *For the border you will have to figure out the quantity of wool you will need after you decide what size the rug will be. Measure the strips for the border in accordance with instructions on page 134. 1 strand of rug wool covers about 1 square inch on #5 canvas.*

Instructions

Bind the edges of the canvas with masking or adhesive tape. With a waterproof marker, make a 9-inch square outline in the center of the canvas.

It is easiest to work the ribbon design first and then fill in the

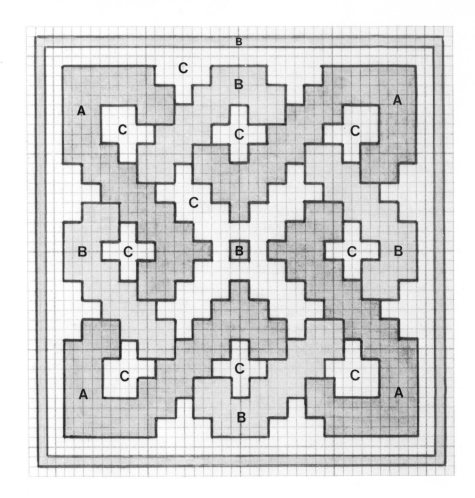

background. Following the chart, work in half-cross stitch as follows: Start with the green yarn in the upper left-hand corner of the 9-inch square. Bring the needle up from the back through the 4th hole down and the 4th from the left. Leave an inch or so of wool at the back to be locked in by your first few stitches.

Insert the needle into the adjacent large hole to the upper right, and bring it out in the large hole directly below (#5 mesh is a double-thread canvas, but you ignore the smaller openings). Continue the half-cross stitch for 10 stitches, as shown on the chart.

Invert the canvas, and work 10 half-cross stitches on the 2nd row.

Invert the canvas and stitch 12 stitches, as shown on the chart. Continue counting and stitching until both the green and orange ribbon designs have been completed. Then fill in the background and the orange outline.

Finishing

After you have completed the number of squares required to form the size rug you want, finish each square separately. Block each square so that it is in the true shape. (See page 55.) Trim unworked canvas margins to 1 inch all around. Snip out a 1-inch square from each corner, being careful not to cut into the needlepoint. Turn the margin to the back, leaving one unworked mesh (thread) all around the edges. Stitch the folded-back margin to the back of the needlepoint by hand. The squares can then be joined together with a connecting row of needlepoint, matching stitch for stitch.

The border can be worked in 4 long strips: 2 strips (the side borders) the length of the squares sewn together, and 2 strips (the end borders) the width of the squares sewn together, plus the width of both side borders. The finished borders should be about 3 inches wide. Cut the strips of canvas to allow a 2-inch margin all around. Borders can be pieced together the same way squares are sewn together, in case you need a longer length than your canvas allows. The side borders of the rug should be cut lengthwise from the canvas, and the end borders should be cut horizontally across the canvas. In this way you can be sure that the warp threads (the two vertical threads that are closest together) are in a vertical position, as they should be.

Use the half-cross stitch. Work the two side borders and the two end borders so that your stitches slant in the same direction as they do on the rug squares.

Work the side borders first—the 2 rows that will be nearest the rug in orange, and 5 rows on the outside edge in green. Snip off the tag ends of colored wool on the back. Then fill in the remaining rows in white.

Refer to the chart on the next page to work the end borders so that the colored rows meet in the finished border.

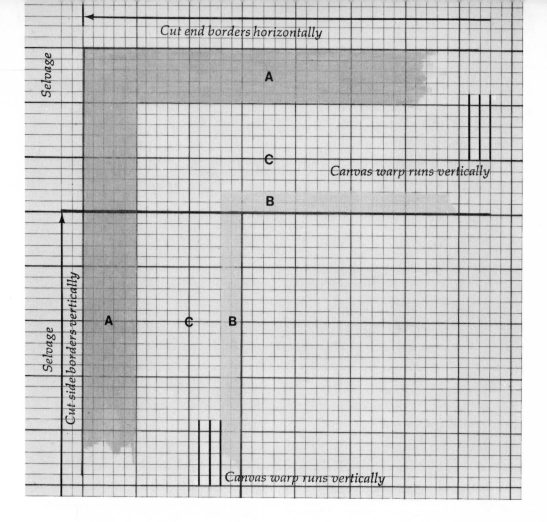

Finishing the Border

After the border pieces are blocked, trim the unworked canvas margins on the orange side of each piece to 1 inch. Then trim the unworked canvas at the ends of the two shorter pieces (the end borders) to 1 inch. Leave the 2-inch unworked margins on the green side (the outside edge) of each border piece, as they will be finished last.

Turn the trimmed margins to the back, leaving one unworked thread of the canvas all around. Stitch these margins to the back of the needlepoint by hand. Join the four border pieces to the body of the rug by the same method as you used to join the squares. Then join the border pieces, where they meet, in the same way.

To finish the outside edge, fold back the unworked 2-inch margin all around so that the last row of needlepoint is at the very edge. Stitch the margin to the back of the needlepoint by hand. Bind the raw edges on the back with rug binding tape or iron-on tape.

134

Index